CHICKEN LITTLE, TOMATO SAUCE AND AGRICULTURE

Who Will Produce Tomorrow's Food?

TOES BOOKS

The Other Economic Summit (TOES) is a forum for the presentation, discussion, and advocacy of the economic ideas and practices upon which a more just and sustainable society can be built—"an economics as if people mattered."

TOES/North America is part of an international network of independent but cooperating initiatives. Those active in TOES/NA are convinced that promising and constructive alternatives are being developed and implemented all over the globe. An economics that more effectively promotes respect for the natural world and realization of human dignity *is* possible. It is the goal of TOES to promote its further conceptualization and to encourage its elaboration in practice.

TOES Books are an initiative of TOES/North America. These books do not represent a TOES position on issues on the TOES agenda but rather seek to further dialogue on and increase understanding of those issues.

CHICKEN LITTLE, TOMATO SAUCE AND AGRICULTURE

Who Will Produce Tomorrow's Food?

Joan Dye Gussow

A TOES Book

The Bootstrap Press
New York

The Bootstrap Press is an imprint of the Intermediate
Technology Development Group of North America,
Inc., 777 United Nations Plaza, New York, New York
10017 (212/953-6920)

Library of Congress Cataloging-in-Publication Data:

Gussow, Joan Dye.
    Chicken Little, tomato sauce and agriculture : who will
produce tomorrow's food? / Joan Dye Gussow.
        p.   cm. — (A TOES book)
    Includes bibliographical references.
    ISBN 0-942850-32-7
    1. Sustainable agriculture—United States. 2. Agriculture—
United States. 3. Food supply—United States. 4. Food industry
and trade—United States—Quality control. I. Title. II. Series.
S441.G87 1991
363.19'2—dc20   91-8899
                                                  CIP

Cover design by Alan Gussow
Typeset and printed in the United States of America

CONTENTS

*To Robert Rodale,
who never ceased believing things could be better
and never stopped working to make them so.*

PROLOGUE: IN THE GARDEN

June. The peas did badly this spring. There has been too much cold rain for the rest of us and I had imagined this would please the peas since they do not like it hot and dry. But most of the seeds never came up to see what the weather would be like, and the green beans are being nipped at the neck before they manage to push their bulky heads through the surface of the soil. The carrots and melons look fine (though I thought melons *hated* cool wet summers) and the potatoes, quite inexplicably, are flourishing. We'll be eating lots of potatoes this winter.

Growing food year after year—trying to develop one's capacity to produce some of what one consumes—is very humbling. My husband said the other day—as we stood contemplating the irrational vigor of the pepper plants in one bed and the sad refusal to thrive of those in another—"It would be very hard to be a farmer."

In a rush, then, one understands how appealing it has been over the last few centuries to fancy that we could profitably eliminate all this variability. How seductive to believe that we could get everything under control once and for all if we only kept trying. Imagine driving the plants to uniform prodigies of production with fertilizers and hormones while simultaneously eliminating their competitors with weed killers and destroying their insect and disease pests with appropriately structured biochemicals. How inescapable has been the temptation, as we face the unpredictability of living things, to succumb to fantasies of absolute control: Mother Nature bound, gagged and blindfolded, helpless at last. Food produced entirely by the wit of man.

Our immediate neighbor's longing for such absolute control came close to impinging on our garden this year when, determined to eliminate "once and for all" the gypsy moth larvae which last year caused some damage to his overcrowded woodlot, he hired a local pest-control company to deliver at high pressure into the tops of his trees the currently allowable concentration of the currently allowable pesticide. His trees are, as it happens, just across the street from our pesticide-free vegetable garden.

This was the second year of the local gypsy moth invasion and our own unsprayed oak trees (which had lost some foliage last year) showed scarcely a sign of damage this year. The few visible larvae hung limply in inverted V's, apparent victims of one of nature's control systems, a bacterial wilt disease. Since our neighbor's trees are no more than 25 feet from ours, it was hard to imagine that his needed spraying. But apparently fearing a reinvasion and, unwilling to take a chance on nature, he put his faith in scientific pest control.

Science was represented in this case by a shirtless youth who, oblivious to whatever warnings might have been printed on the label, was drenching himself and the trees just as we stepped outside to eat dinner on our porch. Having dashed out to warn the sprayer in vigorous terms to direct his spray away from our vegetables, we sat and watched tensely as the milky plume hissed about among the topmost leaves of the trees just across the street. There was an odor of violence being done.

1.

WHAT'S GONE WRONG
WITH OUR FOOD?

In Frederick Pohl's 1952 science fiction classic *The Space Merchants,* the "hero" Mitchell Courtenay begins the book as an advertising man destined for greatness on a depleted planet (ours), where the fires of material desire have been stoked red hot by the arts of commercial persuasion. Early in the book, Courtenay reflects on the nature of the enemy.

> The conservationists were fair game, those wild-eyed zealots who pretended modern civilization was in some way "plundering" our planet. Preposterous stuff. Science is *always* a step ahead of the failure of natural resources. After all, when real meat got scarce, we had soyaburgers ready. When oil ran low, technology developed the pedicab. I had been exposed to Consie sentiment in my time and the arguments had all come down to one thing: Nature's way of living was the *right* way of living. Silly. If "Nature" had intended us to eat fresh vegetables, it wouldn't have given us niacin or ascorbic acid (Pohl and Kornbluth, 1952, 1985).

Later in the book, shanghaied to Costa Rica, Courtenay encounters one of the products that has kept his civilization "a step ahead of the failure of natural resources." He finds himself assigned to skimming chlorella algae to feed, among other things, "Chicken Little," a legless, wingless, headless, featherless technological triumph, a giant mass of

1

flesh "fed by dozens of pipes" from which daily slices are cut to feed a populace otherwise reduced to soyaburgers.

It is evidence of the pace of what is called "progress" that Chicken Little has been transformed in less than four decades from a hideous creature of science fiction to a potentially toothsome product of modern technology. Commenting on consumer resistance to "warmed over flavor" in meat products, the scientist authors of a recent paper on the efficiency potential of a biotechnologically restructured food system note that "single components of animal products should be no more difficult to produce biotechnologically than those from plant products. It is possible that culture of animal organs in vitro may require less time to attain than plant organs, since there is more basic knowledge of animal biochemistry and physiology than there is of plant biochemistry" (Rogoff and Rawlins, 1987). Nor would consumers be limited in this biotechnological paradise to chicken flesh. Brian Stableford in his celebratory *Future Man* imagines not only rows of Chicken Littles fed and purged of wastes through tubes, but also "'neck chops' of lamb on an infinite production line, with red meat and fat attached to an ever-elongating spine of bone" (Stableford, 1984).

Is there a Chicken Little in our future? This book raises the very real possibility that there is one, and urges that this prospect be taken seriously and debated. One possible terminus of the road to the future that we have embarked on has been vividly described. Only by confronting the forces driving us toward such a final destination will we win the chance to become co-planners of a sustainable food system and not mere "planees," adapting to someone else's vision of food system sustainability.

The Food System and the Consumer

In 1985 Kellogg Foundation President Russell Mawby wrote:

> ... few issues are of greater importance to the world than adequate food supplies, proper food use, and knowledge about the components of the agricultural industry. Yet today most people ... do not understand the complexities of America's food system; nor do they fully comprehend its relationship to human nutrition or its impact on international trade relations" (Mawby, 1985).

The thought conveyed by that quotation, that most eaters know dangerously little about agriculture, came forcibly to mind sometime later when a former student forwarded a Del Monte ad from *Family Circle* magazine. On the left-hand page was a full-sized picture of a farmer in plaid shirt and jeans—one of those generic farmers with a big red barn full of hay, chickens out behind the house, a pig in a pigpen, a farm wife in the kitchen. The headline on the facing page read, "Help Keep America Growing." Under it was a button declaring, "I support Farm Aid." The ad copy suggested that if a reader mailed in 20 labels from Del Monte or Hawaiian Punch fruit products, Del Monte would send a dollar to Farm Aid.

FOOD AND MONEY

Economics is linked to food and sustainability in many ways:

1) Since it costs money to buy food, incomes must be high enough so all those who cannot grow food can afford to buy it.

2) Food will only be produced if farmers are paid enough to continue producing it.

3) Poor people pay their debts by producing what rich people will buy. Often this is food.

But food is more important than money. King Midas, after all, starved to death because he got his wish that everything he touched would turn into gold.

4) Food can only be produced anywhere if the flows of energy and materials through the biosphere—nature's "free services that support food production—are sustained. So when "efficiency" (the largest yield per unit of labor) and "lowest cost" are the only goals, producing food means utilizing the products of the land as cheap raw materials to be turned into "food" by modern industrial processing. As raw materials production is moved around the world to where land and labor are cheapest, local economics and ecologies are destroyed for "economic" reasons.

Now the success of that advertisement depends on people being totally ignorant of "the complexities of America's food system." It relies on people being utterly unable to make connections between the state of food and the state of agriculture. Anyone who could make such connections would understand that buying Hawaiian Punch products (made largely from water and limited amounts of, no-doubt, imported fruit juice) is unlikely to do much for the income of the U.S. farmer.

Del Monte was counting here on the fact that the realities of agriculture are invisible to the great majority of food consumers. It is true that several years ago the population generated a brief flurry of concern when actresses Sally Field and Jessica Lange were almost simultaneously threatened with the losses of their cinematic farms. But like the brief wave of interest in supporting the Contras that followed Ollie North's testimony, public awareness of, or concern about, the fate of food producers rapidly became just one more abandoned scrap of yesterday's news. Most inhabitants of the piece of North America called the United States are more than one generation removed from a farm. Their closest connection with the food system occurs in a supermarket, and only those at least a half-century old have ever seen a supermarket stocked predominantly with basic products of plant and animal agriculture.

At the end of World War II, a typical supermarket offered roughly 1,000 items, largely fresh, cured or canned commodities. In the post-war period, however, the simultaneous availability of, among other stimuli, new processing technologies developed for wartime feeding emergencies, suburbs full of housebound women working on a baby boom as well as a new advertising medium—television—stimulated an outpouring of manufactured foods. By the 1980s the number of food products in the supermarket had doubled, redoubled and redoubled again. New introductions in 1989 totalled over 12,000, that is, 33 new products or product variations a day (Shapiro, 1990). Since most of these have little visible connection to the soil, younger Americans can surely be forgiven if they know little, and care less, about how their food gets to the storerooms of supermarkets, the back rooms of *bodegas* or the kitchens of fast (or slow) food restaurants.

Increasingly, moreover, the items available to eat (a frozen pizza, for example) are made up of substances, the sources of which even those ancients familiar with traditional food can hardly imagine. As we once learned, flour comes from milling wheat, tomato paste from crushing vine-grown processing tomatoes, mozzarella from milk and sausage from grinding up and curing various parts of an animal most people

100% PURE APPLE JUICE
PURCHASED IN THE APPLE-GROWING
STATE OF NEW YORK

CONTAINS CONCENTRATE FROM W. GERMANY AUSTRIA, ITALY, HUNGARY AND ARGENTINA
INGREDIENTS: WATER, CONCENTRATED APPLE JUICE

prefer not to reflect upon. In point of fact, however, the flour may be a mix of soy and wheat restructured chemically in order to improve its functional properties, the tomato paste may have been "extended" with colored starch, the mozzarella may be a vegetable oil imitation product and the pepperoni may have been made—without animal contact—from textured soy protein.

While some of these mock animal foods may be less resource intensive than their "real" counterparts, this confounding of foods derived directly from agricultural raw materials with foods created in a sense *de novo* obviously contributes to consumer confusion about the food supply, and will inevitably contribute to an increasingly radical disconnection between the foods people eat and the raw materials produced by farmers.

The passing decades can only exaggerate this disconnection if consumers continue to be more avidly eager for "convenience," novelty and, of late, magically protective components in their foods rather than wholesomeness and recognizability. The substitution of "heating" for "cooking" is proceeding apace. All kitchen appliances with the exception of the microwave are used less each year. The current projection is that 80 percent of American households will have microwave ovens early in this decade, and the food industry is rushing to fill these with microsnacks, TV dinners and one-handed foods designed for busy people. These individualized products are almost inevitably heavily packaged and therefore astonishingly resource intensive in relation to the actual food value they contribute to the diet. Perhaps the most notable recent contribution to this category was Campbell's "Souper Combo," which was featured appropriately in the first issue of the new magazine *Garbage* as providing its purchaser with 11.9 ounces of edible material in six layers of disposable wrapping (In the Dumpster, 1989).

Will Fear Drive Product Reform?

Will consumers continue to buy into such resource-heedless novelty? Looking at present consumer anxieties about food safety, some observers believe that they will not. And it is undoubtedly true that consumers concerned not just about convenience, but about the healthfulness of what they eat, have found the last quarter century or so very disturbing. In the decade immediately following the end of World War II, only a few "faddist" voices questioned the value of the array of new and convenient food products that seemed designed to free women from the kitchen (Rasmussen, 1965). But by the late 1960s, anxieties about the wholesomeness of the U.S. food supply were provoked by what seemed an ever more rapid multiplication on food labels of new and mysterious ingredients with long chemical names. Encouraged by "health food" advocates, growing numbers of what was called the "counterculture" rejected what they viewed as "plastic" supermarket foods and flocked to newly enlarged health or natural food stores (Ullrich, 1972; Belasco, 1989). This was the era during which establishment nutritionists began to worry about dietary fat and heart disease while the counterculture (largely made up of people too young for heart disease) worried more about their conviction that profit-hungry food manufacturers were lacing the food supply with cancer-causing additives. Spurred on by advocacy groups, the FDA managed to publicly banish a few questionable additives, even as hundreds of new ones slipped quietly into the food supply. So the most concerned consumers tried to avoid processed foods and ate "natural" ones.

Hard on the heels of the additive scare came the food scare. The pure food seekers had turned to whole foods, but some of those weren't so hot either. Quiche, even homemade quiche, was not a healthful substitute for Ring Dings. Both of them had too much fat, and fat was implicated not only in heart disease, but in cancer as well. In the early 1980s, the National Academy of Sciences released its report, *Diet, Nutrition and Cancer* (National Research Council, 1982). Although one recommendation urged the FDA to minimize food contamination, most of its advice had nothing to do with additives (at least partly because so little was known about their safety) and everything to do with whole foods.

The report's advice—subsequently reinforced by recommendations from the American Cancer Society and the National Cancer Institute—was to eat more fruits, vegetables and whole grains while consuming less fat (meaning less meat and full-fat dairy products) and more chicken and fish. But for the bewildered consumer, the mandate to eat whole foods arrived in the midst of a food company campaign touting health and nutrition, coupled with a new set of concerns over the very foods being recommended.

With the aging of the baby boomers, it became apparent that nutrition would be "in" with at least one market segment, and the food companies dedicated themselves enthusiastically to profiting from consumer anxiety and confusion over food (Belasco, 1989). Supermarket shelves became filled with products labeled "LITE" and "Natural," and although the meanings of these words were obscure even to those who used them, they gave an impression guaranteed to appeal to consumers' apparent willingness to buy foods that could be perceived as healthier. At one point, the Federal Trade Commission, worried over the misuse of such terms, noted that such products as "natural" margarine, "natural" instant bouillon, "natural" yoghurt chips, "natural" lemon creme (not *cream*) pie and even "natural" cigarettes could be found in supermarkets (FTC . . ., 1978).

As the decade of the 1980s passed its midpoint, science—and world events—further muddied the food safety waters. A few headlines from major stories that appeared in the *New York Times* in the first six months of 1987 help to explain consumers' growing anxiety and confusion.

In April of 1987, Jane Brody, writing under the headline, "New Index Finds Some Cancer Dangers Are Overrated and Others Ignored," described one scientist's ranking system for carcinogens. The system claimed to show that one peanut butter sandwich a day carried ten times the cancer risk of eating three and one-half ounces of cooked bacon. (Three and one-half ounces is eight slices, the equivalent of more than half a pound of [raw] bacon a day—or four pounds a week; a health-conscious consumer who rightly worried about her fat and salt intake would be justifiably baffled) (Brody, 1987a). Brody's follow-up column on the Human Exposure Dose/Rodent Potency, or HERP index, clearly showed tap water to be more dangerous than PCBs, EDBs and DDT (Brody, 1987b).

Three weeks later, women received the bad news that they must avoid even a trace of alcohol. The carryover story in the *New York Times* was headed, "Drinkers Warned on Breast Cancer" (Wilford, 1987). But "drinkers" as it turned out included even Aunt Minnie who only sipped the wine at mass. National Institutes of Health researchers were reported to have found that "*any* amount of alcohol, even the equivalent of less than one drink weekly, raises the breast cancer risk by at least 40 percent" (Edwards, 1987). So for the female consumer in the spring of 1987, water, alcohol and milk fat appeared to be no less dangerous than DDT, suggesting that—at the least—pesticides were safer than we thought.

That news, however, might not have been enough to reassure consumers who learned in the following weeks about two reports from the National Academy of Sciences. The first (Molotsky, 1987) found chemical and microbial contamination of poultry to be widespread; the second (Shabecoff, 1987) found pesticide regulation spotty at best. The riskiest foods, according to the pesticide report, were tomatoes, potatoes, beef, oranges, lettuce, apples, peaches, pork, wheat, soybeans,

© King Features Syndicate. Reprinted with special permission.

Jim Borgman
The Cincinnati Enquirer

carrots, chicken (again), corn and grapes. Obviously a daunting list to those consumers who were trying—as recommended—to eat more fruits, vegetables, grains . . . and poultry. Consumers could learn from the Shabecoff story in the *New York Times* about the NAS pesticide report that 8.75 of 10,000 of them who ate tomatoes over a theoretical 70-year lifetime would "develop cancer from pesticide residues." These stories, discussed at length in the *New York Times,* were reported elsewhere in much less careful detail and, hence, in more alarming shorthand.

Meanwhile millions of Americans watched on "60 Minutes" as machine-eviscerated chickens floated around in a cooling bath contaminated with their own feces; scientists from the Centers for Disease Control in Atlanta announced that occasionally fatal outbreaks of salmonella poisoning had been meticulously traced to hamburger from cattle fed on antibiotic-laced feed (Spika, 1987); and outbreaks of food poisoning around the country caused by unfamiliar names like *camphylobacter* and *listeria* aroused concern even at the FDA, since they raised the possibility that bacteria were learning to survive processing temperatures just as they had learned to flourish on a diet containing antibiotics (New Bacteria . . . 1986). In New York State, among other places, women of childbearing age were being warned on licenses issued to fisherfolk not to eat the catch from many of the state's lakes and rivers (New York State Health Department, 1986). The East Coast shellfish industry was swept repeatedly by unexplained plagues (Du-Pont, 1986; Marcus, 1986; Shell Bacteria, 1988), and as dead dolphins washed onto the Jersey shore, the public became understandably uneasy about eating fish taken from these very same waters.

So bad had things become that America's Personal Health optimist, Jane Brody, wrote in September: "It is easy to see why people are not sure what to eat to lower their risk of cancer or to ward off its spread or recurrence.... Sometimes the very foods suggested as beneficial ... have later been denounced as contaminated with cancer-causing chemicals" (Brody, 1987c).

The year 1988 was a little better. The most popular food component was a healthy one—oat bran—although consumers were appropriately confused about just how much oat bran was enough to free them from the threat of high cholesterol. (Their confusion was helped along, once more, by food manufacturers who brought out products like oat bran spiked donuts.) The news that uncracked eggs were contaminated with salmonella landed softly because a lot of people had already given up eggs on other grounds (St. Louis, et al., 1988), but 1989 came in with a bang. By mid-March, two Chilean grapes laced with cyanide, and a National Resources Defense Council report on possible excessive exposure of children to pesticide residues, had caused a fruit-buyers' panic (NRDC, 1989). It was an actress who riveted public attention on the issue. On "60 Minutes," Meryl Streep told a generation of young professionals that the apple juice with which they were filling their babies' bottles might very well contain hazardous levels of an agricultural chemical by the trade name of Alar.

By the end of March, the cover stories on the two major news magazines asked the questions they thought were most on consumers' minds: "How Safe Is Your Food?" or, even more starkly, "Is Anything Safe?" (*Newsweek* and *Time,* March 27, 1989). On April 5, a full page advertisement in the *New York Times* placed by ACSH (American Council on Science and Health), a strongly pro-business group that sports an impressive scientific advisory board, declared defensively: "OUR FOOD SUPPLY IS SAFE!," followed by a condemnation of "certain environmental groups" for spreading fear "and needless anxiety."

No wonder, then, that when various interested parties surveyed consumers, they found 75 to 90 percent of their respondents expressing concern over residues of pesticides and herbicides. No wonder that the citizens of the nation's dominant agricultural state, frustrated by the

Wellness Update: Thirty-year-old man starting on the twenty-five-thousand-pound oat-bran muffin he must consume over forty years in order to reduce significantly his risk of death from high cholesterol

Drawing by D. Reilly; © 1989 The New Yorker Magazine, Inc.

slow enforcement of their 1987 Safe Drinking Water and Toxic Enforcement Act, put on their 1990 ballot an even more stringent measure, the California Environmental Protection Act of 1990—dubbed "Big Green"—that would, among other things, have phased out 19 agricultural chemicals believed to cause cancer or birth defects (Vaupel, 1989; Reinhold, 1990). Although food safety concerns helped put the measure on the ballot, its defeat at the polls after a big business-financed blitz

(Brooks and Furlong, 1990) sent a confusing message, since the "unbelievably long and overcomplicated" measure (Pear, 1990) included prohibitions against offshore oil drilling and redwood cutting, and a 40 percent reduction in CO_2 emissions, in addition to the pesticide provisions.

Is Anything Wrong with the Food Supply?

Before we begin to ask how these consumer fears might affect the food system, it is essential to point out that where safety is concerned, the present food supply is probably both worse and better than it seems. On the worse-than-it-seems side, control over contamination is either questionable or clearly inadequate along the entire length of the food chain. In 1985, for example, the head of the Bureau of Veterinary Medicine of the FDA testified to Congress that the regulation of animal drugs (residues of which sometimes turn up in meat) was out of control; the bulk of the 20-30,000 drugs in use were not even listed (that is, known to) the FDA. Obviously, under the circumstances, no one was looking for their residues in food (US House, 1985).

A year later, the General Accounting Office reported that an infinitesimal part of the produce grown in the U.S., and only marginally more of the produce grown in tropical countries (where pesticides are often both more poorly regulated and more frequently used), is ever tested for pesticide residues. When residues *are* found in the small proportion of produce tested, the contaminated lot is almost certain to have been already sold to consumers (US GAO, 1986 a, b).

Moreover, it is a fact that as the burdens placed on the regulatory agencies by the pace of chemical innovation have grown, the agencies' resources for enforcing the existing regulations have failed to increase or have actually declined (US GAO, 1990d). A 1989 report from the House Energy and Commerce Subcommittee entitled "Hard to Swallow" noted that just over 2 percent of the 30 billion pounds of food annually imported into the U.S. was physically tested by the FDA for residues or other contamination, and 40 percent of *that* failed to meet FDA standards (US House, 1989). "At present," commented Committee Chair John Dingell (D-MI), "the FDA's ability to prevent contaminated food from reaching the consumer appears at best to be marginal." An FDA spokesperson responded that the system was indeed "strained" and noted that Congress had been told repeatedly of the FDA's need for more resources (Hard to Swallow, 1989).

However, despite these accumulating (and legitimate) causes for concern, things are also better than they seem. Life expectancy in the United States continues to edge up and deaths from heart disease have been declining for several decades. There is no epidemic of cancer; rates at most sites have been fairly constant over a number of years. The exceptions are lung cancer pushed up by smoking, especially among women ("you've come a long way baby"), increased skin cancer reflecting increased UV exposure, and stomach cancer which has been declining for years for reasons that are not entirely clear—although it may be because we eat less moldy food. In other words, surprising as it may seem to a generation weaned on food alarms, there is no clear evidence that anything that has happened in industrializing the food system has harmed us. That's the good news.

It must be noted, however, that our somewhat improved health statistics cannot be used to assuage entirely food safety concerns, since advanced medical technologies are saving many formerly unviable infants at the beginning of life, and early case findings and improved life-extension technologies are prolonging our terminal illnesses. Moreover, even the most reassuring possible life-expectancy statistics cannot be expected to comfort consumers if the agrifood system—continuing down its present path—churns up more accidental industrial contaminations, more outbreaks of new bacteria, more scares about pesticide residues, more dead fish and more warnings against consuming live ones. The 1988 Report of a Food Safety Workshop convened by the industry-defending Institute of Food Technologists concluded that "the American food supply is amongst the safest in the world"* (IFT, 1989). But it will clearly take more than professional spin control to assuage consumer concerns about the wholesomeness of what the agrifood system offers them to eat.

What concerns us here, however, is not the truth or falsity of consumer perceptions about the safety of our food supply, but what kinds of effects those perceptions might have on the food production system. Consumer anxiety, fueled by newspaper headlines and news magazine cover stories, is clearly capable of creating pressures for change at the demand end of the food system. At least some of the consumers, who

---

* It is worth noting that the precise formulation here—"*amongst the safest* in the world"—departs from the standard assertion that we have "the *safest* most abundant food supply in the world." Given the high standards of certain of our European friends, this new modesty is probably appropriate.

have until now appeared content with the marketplace's growing emphasis on convenience and novelty, have become alarmed enough about the *safety* of what there is to eat to demand food that *seems* safer, for example, foods that are certified organic or chemical-free.

Although most consumers, even alarmed consumers, remain ignorant of the functioning of the system that produces what they eat, nagging worries about the wholesomeness of what appears in the supermarkets are exerting pressures on an agricultural system already under stress. For at the other end of the food pipeline—in the farm fields—a different set of problems has begun to prod farmers away from high input industrial farming toward systems of agriculture that will produce the very kinds of foods consumers are demanding. Since many of these farmer problems—ecological as well as economic and political—have been widely publicized, we discuss them only briefly in the following chapter before we return to examining the possible impact of consumer concerns. Chapter 2 begins with a long-range forecast about our agricultural future.

2.

TROUBLES DOWN ON THE FARM

In 1982, an organization called Carrying Capacity, Inc. asked the Complex Systems Research Center of the University of New Hampshire to examine the "carrying capacity" of the United States, that is, to determine whether there were foreseeable limits to the number of people who could continue to be supported at our present lifestyle level by the existing U.S. resource base. Three years later, the result of this ambitious enterprise was published under the title *Beyond Oil* (Gever, Kaufmann, Skole and Vorosmarty, 1986). The researchers had accomplished a task only somewhat less bold than their announced one; they had modeled the U.S. energy future and projected its effect on agriculture over a time span that carried them beyond 2020.

The first part of this chapter, adapted from that book, describes some of the conclusions of the authors and their computer. While the model they used was highly aggregated—that is, all inputs were reduced to energy and land and all outputs to energy—the researchers were able to use the historical record of "how land, energy and energy-based inputs have been used to produce food" in order to calculate "(1) the amount of land and energy needed to meet a specified level of food demand, depending on assumptions regarding erosion, technological change and so on; or alternatively (2) the amount of food that can be produced from a specified amount of land and energy, which are likely to become scarcer as population grows and as oil and gas run out." Here then, are some of their conclusions about the problems and the future of the present system of agriculture. (For a fuller account of how they reached these conclusions, we recommend *Beyond Oil*.)

❖ ❖ ❖ ❖

16

Agriculture: The Exhaustible Cornucopia*

In the opening pages of *The Path to Power,* the first volume of Robert Caro's biography of Lyndon Johnson, Caro called the Hill Country of central Texas in the 1850s "a trap baited with grass." The rolling hills west of Austin were clothed in thick lush grass, which led the first settlers—mostly poor farmers fleeing the worn-out soils of Georgia, Alabama and Tennessee—to believe the Hill Country was a fertile paradise. But the grass "had grown not over a season but over centuries," Caro wrote. "It had grown slowly because the soil beneath it was so thin." Once the grass was stripped away by plows and cattle, nothing was left to anchor the soil. The first few crops were very bountiful, but then the white limestone bedrock began to appear through the soil. Dense brush, previously held in check by prairie fires and the grass, spread over much of the remaining soil. Within a few years, the land that at first had supported huge herds of cattle and bumper crops of corn, wheat and cotton was a virtual desert. Most of those who thought the Hill Country would make them rich instead were condemned—they and generations of their descendants—to lives of grinding poverty. As Caro said, "the Hill Country was hard on dreams."

Today, as government warehouses bulge with surplus food that must be given away or left to rot, it is hard to think of the Texas Hill Country as a microcosm of U.S. agriculture—but that is not far from the truth. Evidence is amassing that indicates that the U.S. agriculture system cannot be sustained in its current form much longer.

Energy and Agriculture

The conventional wisdom about the history of agriculture is marked by misconceptions as to the source of "progress." Typically, American ingenuity and technology are credited with making this nation the World's Breadbasket. In one sense this has been true, but . . . ingenuity and technology have been implemented by funneling ever-increasing flows of fossil fuels into the agricultural system. Take away the fossil fuel subsidies—in the form of tractors, fertilizers, herbicides, insec-

---

* This excerpt adapted from Gever, Robert Kaufmann, David Skole and Charles Vorosmarty, *Beyond Oil. The Threat to Food and Fuel in the Coming Decades.* Cambridge, MA: Ballinger, 1986.

ticides and the other paraphernalia of modern agriculture—and the agricultur[al] system would be lacking virtually everything that makes it more productive than it was in the colonial era. True, the high-yielding crop strains of the Green Revolution have greatly increased per-acre crop yields, and in the laboratory such strains produce more food per unit of fertilizer applied; but over the last 40 years in the real world, these increases have gone hand in hand with even faster increases in the use of energy-based agricultural inputs. The success of U.S. agriculture has relied, and probably will continue for some time to rely, on the heavy use of energy.

The quality of our agricultural resource base has declined just as surely as the quality of our copper resources. Over the last 50 years, the number and size of tractors, the annual use of fertilizers and pesticides and other fuel-based inputs to agriculture have increased much faster than farm output. That is, the energy cost of growing food has been rising. This is partly, perhaps mostly, due to a real decline in the quality of the land we cultivate. Heavy erosion, sinking water tables, pollution and compaction of soil have resulted from the industrialization of agriculture. Along with the conversion of farmland to urban uses, these side effects of industrial agriculture degrade the agriculture resource base. It is difficult or impossible to calculate what fraction of the loss of productivity is due to these effects. But we can be sure that a significant fraction of the increases in energy-based inputs into the agriculture system is needed to make up for resource degradation. We seem to be caught in a vicious circle: intense cultivation techniques are used to make up for the effects of agricultural degradation, but at the same time they worsen that degradation, requiring even more intense cultivation to keep up food output.

The rising domestic demand for crops can be traced both to rising population and to the relatively large proportion of the average diet, about 35 percent of its caloric content, made up of animal products. Nearly 60 percent of our meat, poultry, eggs, dairy products and animal fats come from animals fed on crops rather than grazing land. Based on the proportions of the different kinds of animal-based foods in the average U.S. diet, each kcal of animal-based food requires about 16 kcal (a kcal is the same as a calorie, the familiar measure of food energy) of crops to produce. Not only is there far too little grazing land to accommodate the demand for animal products, but crop-fed animals (especially cattle) generally produce more tender meat than grazed animals do. The end result is that less than one-fifth of the crops grown in the United States for domestic use are eaten directly by people; the vast bulk are fed to cattle, hogs and chickens.

Moreover, when the agriculture system is understood to include the transportation, processing, packaging and distribution of food, it is even more inefficient in terms of edible food energy produced per unit of energy input and even more dependent on energy. About three times as much energy is consumed in these off-farm activities as is used on the nation's farms. Supermarkets across the United States carry oranges, broccoli and other fresh produce, as well as hundreds of kinds of canned and frozen prepared foods, all year long. Many foods that once were prepared at home in a few simple steps now undergo heavy processing before a consumer sees them. The potatoes in Pringle's Potato Chips, for example, are dehydrated, rehydrated, mechanically pressed into a special shape, cooked, packed into a brightly colored container and then shipped to stores across the country. Consumers may enjoy these conveniences, but fossil fuels are required to provide them.

Given the heavy dependence of the agriculture system on fossil fuels and the limits to the nation's energy supplies, we need to ask whether the United States can continue to be the World's Breadbasket. The question is particularly pertinent in light of the importance of food in the nation's trade balance: food exports in 1981 offset half of the dollar cost of imported oil.

The results from the computer model we created help answer that question. The model shows that current trends are not sustainable over the next forty years. We found that the nation can continue to be a net exporter of food only if changes are made in the ways in which food is grown. Either the system must be made more efficient by means such as reducing demand for meats or reversing the ongoing decline in agricultural resource quality, or else an increasing fraction of the nation's scarce fuel supplies will have to be diverted to agriculture from other sectors of the economy. The latter course is extremely perilous: not only would it squeeze manufacturing and service sectors between the rock of agriculture and the hard place of other resource-extraction activities, but it would also entail a further intensification of industrialized agriculture, hastening the long-term decline in the agricultural resource base. Relieving the pressure on the agriculture system might require disagreeable and unpopular sacrifices of cherished eating habits, but failure to make them would jeopardize the entire economy and the long-term ability even to feed ourselves.

The Cost of Maintaining Output

From the 1940s until the late 1970s U.S. agriculture was a story of rising total output, per-acre yields and expectations. During this period most research and effort went toward discovering new ways to use more energy to raise yields. Land was limited and labor was costly, but energy was cheap and abundant.

In the last few years, however, neither output nor the number of people supported by an acre of cropland has risen as fast as before. This has been attributed by some observers to weakened government support for agricultural research (although others have complained about the direction of research as well). Consequently, many scientists and policy people have advocated increased funding for such research, most of which would presumably concentrate on raising per-acre yields. At first glance this seems a laudable goal, as population growth is likely to push the demand for food and fiber upward in the near future. However, our study comes to rather different conclusions.

The quality of the U.S. agricultural resource base has been declining. That is, the amount of food produced per unit of energy has been declining. Three important facts emerge from our analysis: (1) today's methods of farming depend heavily on the use of fossil fuels, especially natural gas and oil products; (2) there are now only very small returns for added energy use; and (3) the amount of oil and gas available domestically is likely to decline before the end of the century.

In the near future farmers will continue to face declining returns on their investment, and in the longer term resource degradation will result in declining absolute returns. If output/input efficiencies keep declining, farmers will achieve high yields only by continuing to make major sacrifices: they will have to pay even more for energy and for all other farm inputs, they will have to accept even lower prices in the market (because of "overproduction"), they will have to live with even lower net returns, and even more of them will go out of business.

It may prove impossible to increase production by increasing the land base or the amount of energy used in farming. It is unlikely that more than 40 or 50 million acres could be added to the current cropland base. Trying to cultivate more land than that would probably reduce the overall average fertility of U.S. farmland, as poorer land would have to be used, and it would reduce the land base available for other vital activities. And using more energy will necessarily reduce the share available to other sectors, which in turn could cause hardships for the agricultural sector because of its links to other sectors. Increasing fuel use in agriculture would also raise the price of fuel. Agricultural policies that emphasize raising production without increasing output/input efficiencies, if they work at all, will be very costly. It seems certain that new, less fuel-intensive methods for producing food will soon be necessary.

The emphasis of policy and research may be better directed toward reducing resource degradation, increasing output/input efficiency and altering cropping practices so that they need less energy. As domestic energy supplies shrink, maintaining production will be a more pressing problem than finding ways to increase it. Fortunately, studies in organic and regenerative farming, integrated pest management and similar approaches suggest that there is much promise in these methods, although much more research is needed.

It is possible to slow erosion greatly and thereby to stop the decline in resource degradation. It is even possible to build up soil organic matter and to *reverse* the decline. Other examples abound, but it is clear that the closer the system is tied to its fossil fuel resources—and the further it is removed from its biological resources—the more likely it is that food production will continue to decline in quality and efficiency.

Will agriculture reverse the trend in declining resource quality? The answer to this question largely depends on our ability to implement appropriate policies. Nonetheless, agriculture is an activity that in its best practices links human knowledge and biological processes. Food is a renewable resource.

❖ ❖ ❖ ❖

This chapter continues with an excerpt from a 1988 report from the Midwestern Legislative Conference, entitled *Prodigal Crops: A Review of Proposals for Sustaining Agriculture,* examines farmer problems and looks at recent moves toward a more sustainable agriculture.

❖ ❖ ❖ ❖

I. BACKGROUND*

A Televised Crisis

Throughout the 1980s, Americans have watched as scenes of agricultural crisis played across TV and movie screens. First, we witnessed news accounts of farm foreclosures and auctions. Then we saw a series of Sissy Spacek-type movies of rural hardships. Finally . . . we watched as farmers on the evening news searched the clear skies for a sign that rains would come to bring life back to parched soil.

A growing number of critics of contemporary conventional American agriculture foresee more ominous scenes on the horizon. Some predict pictures of dustbowl conditions as badly eroded soil blows off the Great Plains. Others see rural versions of the Love Canal as water and soil resources polluted by misuse of chemical fertilizers and pesticides become unusable.

All of these critics, who range from agricultur[al] researchers to farmers to environmentalists, see trouble ahead for American farmers and food producers if steps are not taken to ensure that agriculture in the United States is sustainable for the long run. . . .

A Confluence of Concerns

Rural environmental concerns have come to a critical point in the midst of a widespread farm economy crisis. Farmers across the Midwest are looking for ways to cut costs and to protect the soil from which springs their livelihood. "Do you know a farmer who hasn't tried to cut costs," asks James O. Morgan, Vice President and Executive Director of the Rodale Institute. "One of the costs he can cut is inputs," said Morgan.

Cutting inputs also cuts to the core of environmental concerns. This confluence of concerns has farmers across the country looking for reliable information of ways of lowering inputs while sustaining profitable yields. . . .

---

* This excerpt to end of chapter adapted from *Prodigal Crops: A Review of Proposals for Sustaining Agriculture*. (Emerging Issues Series.) A Report of the Midwestern Legislative Conference of the Council of State Governments, December 1988 (641 East Butterfield Road, Suite 401, Lombard, IL 60148).

Troubling Trends

The environmental, economic and social concerns behind the movement can be glimpsed in a series of statistics that indicate some troublesome trends.

- The United States loses 3.1 billion tons of topsoil annually to erosion (McCullough and Weiss, 1985).

- About 23% of the nation's cropland loses twice the established tolerable amount every year (McCullough and Weiss, 1985).

- Congress estimates off-farm costs of dealing with soil sedimentation at between $2 billion and $6 billion annually (Guither, 1987).

- Fertilizer use in the U.S. increased more than 300% from 1960 to 1980 (Health and Environment Network, January 1988).

- Current fertilizer use amounts to about 40 million tons per year on U.S. fields (Lovins, Lovins and Bender, 1984).

- Pesticide use increased 40-fold between 1950 and 1980. (USDA, 1980)

- Current food production, preparation and distribution systems use 9.8 calories of energy for each calorie of food consumed in the United States (Lovins, Lovins and Bender, 1984).

- Low commodity prices, high debt loads and unstable land prices have placed large numbers of American farmers at risk financially. In January 1986, some 40,000 farms were technically insolvent (Madden, 1987).

- U.S. farm population has decreased from 23 million (or 15.3% of the population) in 1950, to 5.2 million (or 2.2% of the population in 1986) (U.S. Census Bureau).

Critics of conventional agriculture point to these statistics as signs that contemporary American agriculture is not sustainable in the long run. Fertilizers based on fossil fuels cannot be used forever. Soil damaged by misuse of chemicals and by cropping practices aimed at ever-increasing yields cannot produce forever. Water damaged by silt and chemical runoff or leaching cannot support agriculture in the long run.

FIGURE 1: U.S. FARM DEBT 1940-1985
(In billions of $)

	Farm debt outstanding, December 31							
	1940	1950	1960	1970	1980	1983	1984	1985
Real estate debt:								
Federal land banks..........	2.7	1.0	2.5	7.1	36.2	48.8	49.1	44.6
Life insurance companies	1.0	1.4	3.0	5.6	12.9	12.7	12.4	11.8
Banks	0.5	1.0	1.6	3.8	8.6	9.3	10.2	11.4
Farmers Home Administration ..	0.1	0.3	0.7	2.4	7.7	9.5	10.0	10.4
Individuals and others	2.2	2.5	5.0	11.4	30.2	32.3	29.9	27.2
Total...................	6.5	6.1	12.8	30.3	95.8	112.6	111.6	105.4
Nonreal estate debt:								
Banks	1.0	2.5	5.0	11.1	31.6	39.0	39.6	35.5
Production credit associations[1] .	0.2	0.5	1.5	5.3	20.5	20.8	18.8	14.5
Farmers Home Administration ..	0.5	0.3	0.4	0.8	11.8	14.6	15.7	17.1
Individuals and others[2].......	1.7	2.8	5.1	5.1	17.7	18.9	18.0	15.4
Total...................	3.3	6.1	12.0	22.3	81.6	92.8	92.2	82.5
Commodity Credit Corporation ...	0.6	0.8	1.4	1.9	5.0	10.8	8.6	16.9
Total...................	10.5	13.1	26.2	54.5	182.3	216.2	212.3	204.8

[1]Includes loans to other financial institutions (OFL's)
[2]Includes Small Business Administration loans

(Source: United States Department of Agriculture, Office of Governmental and Public Affairs, *1987 Fact Book on U.S. Agriculture,* Washington, DC: USDA, July 1987, p. 17.)

Likewise, farmers crippled by high debt loads will search for ways to get better prices and save on expenses. Those who are unable to manage financially will continue to leave the land and migrate to urban areas.

What Is Sustainable Agriculture?

The combination of economic and environmental issues has made for a problem that "you couldn't produce your way out of," said Professor Dennis Keeney, Director of the Leopold Center for Sustainable Agriculture at Iowa State University.

Keeney foresees a transition in American agriculture from a system predicated on increasing crop production to one focusing on "the appropriate use of crop and livestock systems and agricultural inputs supporting those activities which maintain economic and social viability while preserving the high productivity and quality of . . . land."

That formal definition of sustainable agriculture is contained in the Iowa legislation that created the Leopold Center. However, there are many, sometimes conflicting, notions of what "sustainable agriculture" means. . . .

For Dick Thompson, a farmer in Boone, Iowa, sustainable agriculture refers to "profitability, environment, people and community." Thompson has been successfully farming 300 acres without pesticides or petroleum-based fertilizers for almost 30 years.

"Sustainable agriculture is a holistic system, one that is self-supported by on-farm inputs, looking out for the environment while maintaining profitable yields," said Mike Strohm. Strohm minimizes off-farm, chemical inputs on his 560 acres in West Union, Illinois.

Low-Input Farming

Both Thompson and Strohm probably would agree that their farming systems could be defined under the definition of "low-input" farming provided by Garth Youngberg, Executive Director of the Institute for Alternative Agriculture.

According to that definition, "low-input farming seeks to optimize the management and use of internal production inputs in ways that provide acceptable levels of sustainable crop yields and livestock production and which result in economically profitable returns. This approach emphasizes such cultural and management practices as crop rotations, recycling of animal manures and conservation tillage to control soil erosion and nutrient losses and to maintain or enhance soil productivity. Low input farming systems seek to minimize the use of external production inputs such as purchased fertilizers and pesticides wherever and whenever feasible to lower production costs, to avoid pollution of surface and ground water, to reduce pesticide residues in food, to reduce a farmer's overall risk and to increase both short and long-term farm profitability."

"The idea [is to create] systems tending toward long-term sustainability. But there is no widespread agreement on length. Sustainable implies forever," Dr. Youngberg said.

While this definition of "low-input" makes no mention of social factors, Youngberg cited concerns about the loss of farms and personal health as driving forces behind the increased interest in creating more sustainable systems.

To Save the Family Farm

. . . Sustainable agriculture came out of the drive to preserve moderate- and family-size farms as economically viable and socially desirable, explained Denny M. Caneff, executive director of the Wisconsin Rural Development Center. "Next came the environmental impact. That became the easiest handle to get on sustainable ag. It was easier than asking how to sustain the social aspect or how to provide economic sustainability. . . .

Among the social concerns Caneff and others feel a broadened vision of sustainability would address include:

- Preserving small- and medium-size farms.

- Developing local suppliers of needed inputs and local processors of farm products.

- Keeping more agriculturally produced profit in rural communities and thereby aiding rural economic development.

- Encouraging more owner operation of farms and less corporate ownership of farm land.

- Encouraging community-based solutions to rural health and environmental concerns.

While this agenda is compatible with the more narrow goal of lowering chemical inputs, it also obviously conflicts with the operating principles of those who have no problem with corporate ownership of farmland or those who see no fundamental value in small- or medium-sized farms.

Nonetheless, whether out of the nearly universal desire to cut costs or out of the broader desire to address rural social problems, interest in lowering inputs, preserving the soil and making farming more profitable for the farmers is growing nationwide.

In less than five years, American agriculture has moved from a situation where the words "sustainable agriculture" were met with at best a blank stare, and at worst open hostility, to a situation where farmers from the smallest part-time operators to some of the largest ranchers are using a variety of low-input techniques and eagerly seeking information on more of the same.

II. TECHNIQUES

High Yield Research

Conventional American agriculture in the post World War II era has emphasized and achieved continuously increasing crop yields. Agriculture research has centered on developing new technologies, equipment and inputs to achieve the desired yields.

The development of fossil fuel-based fertilizers and chemical pesticides along with the design and production of larger and more complex farm machines have driven the yields to their current levels. Farm policy has encouraged ever larger yields and farm technology has made them possible. Today's farmer can plant a single crop from fence to fence, spray it and harvest it using huge and expensive machinery to accomplish each task more quickly than farmers from just 40 years ago would ever have thought possible.

Simplified, contemporary conventional grain farming techniques consist of:

* Preparing the soil using inputs and machinery.

* Perhaps using a conservation tillage method (minimum till or no-till) combined with high levels of pesticides.

* Planting vast amounts, usually of corn or soybeans, in a method known as monocropping.

* Spraying the entire crop at intervals recommended by the spray manufacturers.

* Harvesting another bumper crop using a massive combine.

This cycle is repeated year in and year out across the great grain-producing Heartland of the country and has been for four decades. With inputs costing a farmer with a medium-size spread $15,000-20,000 annually and specialized farm equipment costing up to four times that amount, contemporary chemical intensive agriculture is also capital intensive.

Making the soil ready, planting the right seeds at the right time, providing soil nutrients, protecting the crop from weeds and other pests and then harvesting has been the method and challenge for farmers since agriculture began. Conventional farming uses high input levels to accomplish these fundamental goals. Alternative agriculture uses other methods.

In its 1980 *Report and Recommendations on Organic Farming,* USDA defined organic farming as "a production system which avoids or largely excludes the use of synthetically compounded fertilizers, pesticides, growth regulators and livestock feed additives. To the maximum extent feasible, organic farming systems rely upon crop rotations, crop residues, animal manures, legumes, green manures, off-farm organic wastes, mechanical cultivation, mineral-bearing rocks, and aspects of biological pest control to maintain soil productivity and tilth, to supply plant nutrients and to control insects, weeds and other pests" (USDA, 1980).*

A Systems Approach

Perhaps the most important component in the USDA definition is the term "production system." Sustainable agriculture emphasizes a systems approach to farming. . . .

"A farming *system* is not just a simple sum of all of its components but rather a complex system with Intricate Interactions" (Edwards, 1987). Conventional farming can achieve high yields without attending to these interactions. Added pesticides will get rid of the pests and diseases invited by the lush growth resulting from heavy fertilizer. "However, as chemical inputs are lowered progressively, so the need for attention to the mechanism by which one input impacts upon another increases" (Edwards, 1987).

This systems approach makes it impossible to produce a simple

---

* Organic farming has since taken on a more precise legal definition in a number of states and it usually excludes all chemical pesticide use. . . . What USDA described in 1980 as "organic" has come to be called low-input or low-input sustainable agriculture. While acknowledging the differences of opinion surrounding the definition of sustainable agriculture for the purposes of discussing actual agriculture techniques and methods, the USDA definition of organic farming is suitably precise also to define sustainable agriculture.

"how to" guide directing a farmer to take step A for cultivation, step B for fertilization and step C for crop protection. Operating a sustainable system is management intensive requiring an understanding not only of the general interrelationships of basic components, but also an understanding of each in relation to the specific farm situation.

[As essayist, poet and farmer Wendell] Berry has written:

> The good farmer, like an artist, performs within a pattern; he must do one thing while remembering many others. He must be thoughtful of relationships and connections, always aware of the reciprocity of dependence and influence between part and whole. His work may be physical, but its integrity is made by thought. We will not understand what we mean when we say that he works with his hands, if we do not also understand that he works also with his mind . . . (Berry, 1984).

Obviously, low-input, sustainable agriculture practices require long-term planning, high level management skills and a commitment to the future. . . .

As Patrick Madden, Manager of the Cooperative State Research Service Program, USDA, described it:

> . . . [a] low-input/sustainable farming system is a combination and sequence of low-input farming methods or technologies integrated into a whole-farm managerial plan. Many of the concepts underlying low-input farming methods, such as crop rotations and application of manures, have been known for decades or even centuries. However, the essence of this approach is not a reversion to the technologies of previous decades or centuries, but a combination of the best of modern agricultural science and technology with the practical experience of farmers who are profitably substituting management for most or all of their purchased inputs of synthetic chemical pesticides and fertilizers (Madden, 1988).

III. ENVIRONMENTAL CONCERNS

When asked about the increasing interest in sustainable agriculture, Thompson, of Iowa, responded, "Farmers are becoming more concerned about erosion of the topsoil. Some are concerned about groundwater but most don't know what to do about it. Many want to know how to farm without pesticides."

Erosion, groundwater degradation and pesticides are the primary environmental concerns driving farmers to consider farming with fewer chemicals and more concern for protecting natural resources for the future.

Erosion

When the multi-billion dollar off-farm costs of dealing with erosion are factored in, food production in the United States may seem less of a bargain. The cost of clearing ditches and cleaning waterways is a byproduct of an agricultural system that has paid too little attention to the problem of soil erosion.

The 1985 federal farm bill contain[ed] a landmark conservation section aimed at protecting both soil and water resources . . . (USDA, 1985). While most advocates of sustainable farming applaud the federal efforts as a step in the right direction, some have argued that the conservation program does not go far enough and that it has not yet been strictly applied. Others contend that as long as federal farm programs focus primarily on production goals, the environmentally beneficial practices of sustainable agriculture will never receive widespread support. Such practices place a premium on preserving the productivity of the land in the long run as opposed to using techniques that may produce large yields in the short run at the expense of losing soil or degrading water.

In addition to federal conservation programs, various forms of conservation tillage are being used now on many conventional farms as a method of protecting the soil. "[C]onservation tillage is one of the most effective and least expensive methods for controlling soil erosion. When properly applied, it can significantly reduce soil losses" (Papendick, Elliott and Dahlgren, 1986).

However, "[w]ith reduced tillage, farmers may rely more on broad-spectrum herbicides such as glyphosate and paraquat for preplant application. . . . Moreover, the chemicals applied in conservation tillage systems are more likely to remain at the soil surface rather than being incorporated into the soil, a situation which raises questions about the escape of these chemicals into the environment via runoff" (Papendick, Elliott and Dahlgren, 1986). Research concerns center on the potential for leaching and groundwater contamination with minimum till systems (Papendick, Elliott and Dahlgren, 1986).

Groundwater

Groundwater contamination has emerged as the primary rural environmental concern of the late 1980s. With state and federal surveys revealing widespread contamination of well water in several agriculture areas, and with both state and federal agencies responding with tighter restrictions on the offending agriculture chemicals, farmers have become increasingly concerned about long-term prospects for chemical intensive farming.

As a cure for groundwater ills, sustainable agriculture shows promise. Use of the methods described above eliminates many of the offending chemicals and thus sharply reduces the possibility of groundwater contamination.

Pesticides

Discussion about agricultural environmental concerns inevitably revolves around the ubiquitous pesticide issue. In an information pamphlet on pesticides, the American Chemical Society says, "Nearly every sector of our modern society uses pesticides. About one billion pounds of synthetic organic pesticides were produced in the United States in 1985. This quantity represents roughly 50,000 pesticide products based on some 1,400 active ingredients, 600 of which are the most common. Agricultural use accounts for 77% of all pesticides sold in the United States" (American Chemical Society, n.d.).

Yet little is known about the long-term risks of heavy pesticide use. Historically, safety has taken a back seat to production in the introduction of new pesticides. Rather than require that manufacturers prove that a pesticide is safe prior to introducing it, generally a danger has to be proved to have a pesticide removed. Because some effects of long-term exposure to pesticides may not show up for decades, proving a long-term danger is difficult and costly.

With significant exposures in the short term, pesticides "cause cancer and birth defects. Farm workers are at greatest risk, due to direct and prolonged exposure. . . . Strong statistical evidence [suggests] that people living in areas where pesticides are heavily utilized have elevated risk of dying from certain kinds of cancer. . . . Furthermore, as pests develop resistance, pesticides become obsolete. "The cost of developing and gaining approval of new pesticides, already astronomical, is rapidly rising" (Madden, 1988).

As with groundwater contamination, the alternative techniques associated with sustainable agriculture would eliminate pesticide use to a significant degree. Some proponents of sustainable agriculture see a relatively quick and highly significant transformation in American agriculture toward less dependence on chemicals. When asked about the prospects of widespread use of sustainable techniques, Dr. Keeney of the Leopold Center responded, "I think we'll have a fairly chemical-free agriculture in 20 years."

❖ ❖ ❖ ❖

3.

ENVISIONING A FUTURE

As the preceding chapter makes clear, the forces driving change in the agri-food system are not primarily consumers' anxieties over food safety that were sketched out in the first chapter. What is driving change is the reality that the present food production system is proving economically infeasible for many farmers, toxic to the environment and destructive to the farmers' own resource base. How can these sorts of issues—farmers' concerns over production methods and consumers' anxieties over consumption safety—be addressed? As the Governors' *Prodigal Crops* report in Chapter 2 suggests, what is broadly called sustainable agriculture is now being viewed by some sectors of the farm economy as a solution to many of our agricultural problems. Since it is a production method that makes minimal, if any, use of toxic chemicals, it might also be viewed as a potential answer to consumers' concerns over food safety. Can we assume, then, that our food future will involve a relatively "chemical-free" agriculture embedded in a food system that is sustainable in the ways described in the preceding chapter? Is Chicken Little merely a fantasy?

Although there are a number of ways of categorizing views of the future, the one I have found most useful was laid out more than a decade ago by James Robertson in a little book entitled *The Sane Alternative* (Robertson, 1979). He proposed that contemporary views of humanity's probable future could all be classified in one of five ways: Business-as-Usual, Disaster, Totalitarian Conservationist, Hyper-Expansionist (HE) and Sane/Humane/Ecological (SHE). The first two are relatively self-explanatory. When I used to ask my students to predict

33

what would happen to the food system under each of these scenarios, they usually concluded that the first would lead inevitably to the second—that is, Business-as-Usual would lead to Disaster. Where agriculture is concerned the preceding chapters tend to confirm this prediction.

The Totalitarian Conservationist alternative requires somewhat more explaining. This is a future in which the public, terrified by multiplying environmental crises, accepts (or demands) a strong leader who will *impose* restrictions designed to save the globe. Interestingly, this future was usually my (largely female) students' second choice. Their first choice was the Sane/Humane/Ecological or SHE alternative, which seemed most compatible with the future they *wanted* (although they tended to despair of its attainability). The SHE future and its antithesis, the Hyper-Expansionist or HE future, seem to encompass between them most of the "solutions" to the food system crisis currently put forward by forecasters of different philosophical persuasions.

Seeking a "Soft" Path

The Business-as-Usual system referred to above—the food system that is profligate with energy, cropland and water, that produces pesticide-contaminated food, bankrupt farmers, unacceptable levels of topsoil loss, tomatoes more crash resistant than car bumpers (Whiteside, 1977) and 12,000 new products a year—that system is, as the Carrying Capacity analysis shows, clearly leading us rapidly to disaster. One apparent route of escape is the SHE alternative. This is what one might call, after Amory Lovins, a "soft path" system, making use of what Rifkin would term empathetic technologies (Rifkin, 1985). At the end of this path is a food supply made up of whole fresh foods produced by environmentally benign methods somewhere in the vicinity of where they are to be eaten.

Although my own bias in favor of such a future is probably obvious by now, it springs from a hard won conviction that smaller scale, more localized food systems are essential and ultimately inevitable. It daily seems more evident that humans cannot escape—as we have tried to do over the last centuries—being part of nature. As even the popular press has begun to note seriously, the globe is striking back against our assaults. The greenhouse effect, the ozone hole, the loss of tropical forests with their climate control function, our heedless destruction of natural species even before we have discovered their role in holding together the tissue of life—these are but the loudest of many signals that the human species, with its much bragged-about control over nature, is hitting up against some outer limits. The system of which these particular outcomes are symbolic, a system that rewards gigantism and waste in our economic life—and is explicity indifferent to whatever it designates as a "side effect"—this system seems out of control.

There is no evidence, moreover, that the part of this system represented by large scale industrial agriculture and an oligopolistic food system is sustainable over the long term, and there is accumulating evidence that it is not. Moreover, it seems less and less likely that this hyperproductive agrifood system will ever be willing to accommodate itself to the interlocking natural cycles, the continued operation of which is essential for human survival. Therefore, I am convinced that a food-producing system based largely on smaller farms and smaller processors, a system more adapted to local conditions, more responsive to local climate and topography, less polluting of the land, the water and the food it produces, is inevitable. But whether such a system will emerge slowly as society makes a rational transition to sustainability or whether a few remnant farms and small businesses will remain as models for us to examine and to emulate after the economic/ecological collapse toward which business-as-usual is driving us . . . that is a question no one can presently answer.

It has also begun to appear evident to me as a nutrition educator that the only sort of diet realistically possible to recommend to whole populations over the long term would be a diet largely composed of a variety of minimally processed (whole) foods, mainly non-animal products, that have been minimally exposed to pesticides, preservatives, processing aids or other non-food chemicals whether added inadvertently or intentionally. As that list of potential "additives" suggests, such a "natural" diet would probably also make the task of teaching food selection more manageable. We should not expect ordinary people to become chemists and toxicologists in order eat wisely. They should be able to get by knowing merely which *foods* to select. In other words, a supply of whole foods produced by a rational and sustainable system would probably result in a more *intelligible* food supply as well.

Those who believe that parsimony is evidence of truth will be impressed by the fact that these two conclusions mesh nicely. The agricultural system that seems inevitable if U.S. society is to survive in the long run would be capable of providing the kinds of diets that look to be both the most wholesome and the most readily teachable.

"Geoffrey's seasonal. I'm regional."

•   •

Drawing by Victoria Roberts; © 1989 The New Yorker Magazine, Inc.

Among those who share these views, there has been a growing sense of optimism in the past few years that this "soft path" is the one increasingly sought out. Militantly chemical schools of agriculture at the nation's land-grant colleges, long the source of unquestioning support for high tech, high fertilizer, high pesticide cropping have been holding workshops and field days on organic or low-input sustainable agriculture (LISA). Many of them, indeed, are setting up sustainable agriculture programs. In California, the nation's largest agricultural state, University of California–Davis—home of the notorious square (and hard) tomato—has a Sustainable Agriculture Research and Education Program. Once forbidden "hippie" terms like permaculture are discussed at UC–San Diego, and UC–Santa Cruz's once academically disdained on-campus farm has been adopted as the site for a serious investigation of ecologically sound agriculture.

The reasons for this shift in attitude are clear enough. As the two excerpts in Chapter 2 show, the energy crisis of the 1970s brought to light—and subsequent events have further illuminated—the reality that our controlling technologies are failing to keep us "one step ahead" of resource failure. The "consie" propaganda about which Pohl and Kornbluth wrote almost 40 years ago turns out to be true. We *are* "in some way 'plundering' our planet" (Pohl and Kornbluth, 1952). The soft path has been given legitimacy by a series of environmental and farm crises that have resulted from the problems documented earlier: the bankruptcy of small farms and small banks, fertilizer and pesticide pollution of ground water, the salting up of irrigated farmland and so on.

As was also suggested earlier, interest in alternative systems has been economically forced as some farmers, caught between high costs of production and low prices for their products, have sought to reduce costs and hence potentially increase profits by returning to farm-produced animal and green manures instead of purchased petrochemical fertilizers to increase fertility, even as they seek to use less costly and more biologically based methods of pest control. The post-war agronomic dream of achieving total control over nature with modern chemistry seems to be yielding not just to ecological argument, but to economic reality as well.

These pressures, combined with a consumer-instigated demand for "clean, pesticide-free produce," have created a climate in which farmers sense the possibility of making money by practicing a non-chemical agriculture. So on the side of optimism it could be argued, as Chapter 2 indicates, that agriculture is moving toward the soft path, toward a sane/humane/ecological future as a way out of its present dilemma.

The Promise—and Threat—of Biotechnology

But even as interest is growing in relocalizing food systems, and even as a more sustainable agriculture is being widely viewed as offering an escape from many of the problems afflicting our food systems, a new technology is threatening (or promising) to transform agriculture—and society. Viewed from the standpoint of a "soft path" food system, genetic engineering has been widely acclaimed as a potential solution to many of our agricultural problems. With genetic engineering, we are promised, plants can be given the ability to fix their own nitrogen—thus reducing both the demand for petrochemicals and water-polluting nitrogen runoff. Plants can also be made pest resistant (thus eliminating the need for pesticides) and day-neutral, thus extending seasons and ranges. The capacity to make plants drought- or salt-tolerant more rapidly could be an essential one if the threatened Greenhouse warming begins to raise temperatures and sea levels. This has been the promise.

The reality, as has often been pointed out, is quite different. The reality is that among the first commercial agricultural biotech products are herbicide-resistant crop plants, the use of which may well *increase* herbicide use by "matching" the herbicide a company manufactures with its own "resistant" seeds (Goldberg, et al, 1990). Other negative consequences are also possible. As Senator Albert Gore, Jr. warned at an NAS symposium on "Biotechnology and the Food Supply":

> Many fear that the brave new world of biotechnology will also have a dark side. . . . My biggest fear is not that by accident we will set loose some genetically defective Andromeda strain. Given our record in dealing with agriculture, we are far more likely to accidentally drown ourselves in a sea of excess grain (Gore, 1988).

That Gore's concerns may be justified is strongly suggested by another of the early achievements of biotech. Montsanto claims to have invested $300 million in developing Bovine Growth Hormone (BGH)—renamed Bovine Somatotropin (BST) to avoid the "hormone" image problem—a drug that can be injected into dairy cows to increase their milk production (Schneider, 1990a,b). Production of more milk than the food system can absorb has been a chronic problem in the U.S., so much so that in 1985 Congress passed a Dairy Termination Program designed to "terminate, by slaughter or export, whole herds of dairy cattle (US GAO, 1990). It is seas of grain—and of milk—that have throughout our nation's history been the consistent cause of low prices and the farmer's consequent need to produce as much as possible (at whatever cost to the environment) just to pay back the money borrowed to put in a crop.

But this new technology may not just daunt weeds and insects or promote overproduction and farm bankruptcy. It has the potential to thrust us powerfully toward an entirely novel future—toward an agriculture fundamentally different in its structure and assumptions from the one envisioned by the proponents of low-input sustainable farming. For while biotechnology may be capable of enhancing our collective ability to cooperate with nature in the service of human survival, it is equally capable of being utilized by the agrifood industry to further increase its control over the natural world. This latter route of escape from our agricultural dilemmas, Robertson would have characterized as a HE, or Hyper-Expansionist vision. It is a world in which nature's long-term reliability would be replaced by clever technologies promising unparalleled abundance at merely the cost of computerized vigilance. This vision implies systems that will demand the monitoring of fallible sensors by bored humans serving the giant corporations that control the food system.

Dreams of the Future

The futurist literature in agriculture has long been replete with plans for technologies that promise increasing control over what is seen as the unpredictability (read "unreliability") of nature. Twenty years ago, the "Revolution in American Agriculture" that Billard reported in the pages of *National Geographic* celebrated the farmer's increasing energy consumption for harvesting-factories in the field, automated chicken apartment houses and heated farrowing pens for hogs. The pictured farm of the future featured a "modernistic farm house" on which "a bubble-topped control tower hums with a computer, weather reports and a farm-price ticker tape" (Billard, 1970). Fifteen years later, the bubble-topped control tower was anachronistic. The future farmer, featured in Holt's 1985 article "Computers in Production Agriculture" in *Science,* awakens to look at his bedroom computer monitor to read out the condition of his cows and sows who are automatically fed and watered. He proceeds through his day, remotely monitoring everything from soil moisture levels to optimum herbicide delivery times and presumably gets his exercise in a gym (Holt, 1985). The goal underlying these various scenarios—of which these are only the most famous and most quoted—was perfectly described in a *New York Times'* headline for a story describing research underway for Walt Disney's Epcot Center. The headline read, "Outwitting Nature to Produce More Food" (Brody, 1980).

Reading these high tech scenarios, one sometimes has the feeling that their authors actually yearn for the time when we will have been *forced*—by our heedless abuse of natural systems—to grow plants artificially. There is something challenging about designing such a future, with uniformly docile cattle housed in elevated silos, their manure coming down chutes to grow plants hydroponically. It is reassuring to contemplate the promises implied by "The World of the Future" in Epcot Center's The Land exhibit at Walt Disney World in Florida, a technological paradise, where all the variables are *controlled:* the plants held up by mesh rather than messy dirt, the nutrients supplied at *precise* intervals by an *automated* flow-through system, the air *filtered* and *sterilized* to prevent the introduction of insects and diseases. Such visions are reassuringly removed from those awful scenes of starving children on the Ethiopian desert.

Because such ideal systems always appear in isolation from a real world—in which the physical hazards of water shortages, topsoil loss, energy constraints, weeds and insects are multiplied by the social hazards of disorder and strife—they are easy to dismiss as unrealizable fantasies. And while such perfect worlds may indeed be fantasies in the face of the ecological, economic and social realities afflicting the global food system, it is necessary to take much more seriously a very different vision of the future recently proposed by two U.S. Department of Agriculture scientists in a paper entitled "Food Security: A Technological Alternative" (Rogoff and Rawlins, 1987). The authors share the same concerns over the stress that the global food system is placing on the environment as do the advocates of eco-agriculture. But looking seriously at the potential of biotechnology, they come up with a radically different solution. They come up with Chicken Little.

Rogoff and Rawlins conclude, as do the proponents of sustainable agriculture, that even in perennially grain-glutted America the nation's margin of safety is very small: "The existing U.S. food chain could collapse," they write, "as a result of one autumn without a harvest"—a harvest highly dependent on weather, supplies of fossil energy and other resources. In considering how to overcome these threats, the authors begin from the basic fact that agriculture is fundamentally a system to capture solar energy and convey it to humans in the form of edible materials.

The protein, vitamins and minerals humans get from plants (and the animals that eat those plants) are useful to us, and to the plant. But the plant's fundamental role in the human food system is to use solar energy to transform air, soil and water into solids that can be consumed.

Unfortunately, humans cannot digest the majority of what plants make. Most vegetation is made up of perennials—trees, shrubs, grasses—relatively high in materials like cellulose and lignin that must be broken down by gut enzymes. Termites have these enzymes; humans do not. So, over time, our ancestors found and cultivated plants that produced directly consumable parts. Much of what humans could digest were starch-rich plant reproductive organs—grains, fruits, seeds. Annuals require more elaborate reproductive organs just to survive because they have to start growth from seed every year. Thus, many of the crops humans domesticated for food were annuals.

Production of annual plants, however, requires yearly plowing of the soil. This in turn leads to soil erosion, one of the serious problems agriculture now faces. In the article excerpted in the following chapter, Rogoff and Rawlins seek to solve that and other agricultural problems with an entirely novel system—one that is much more "efficient" than our present one in delivering solar energy (in the form of desired end products) to consumers.

4.

PURE FOOD: A TECHNOLOGICAL ALTERNATIVE*

Marin Rogoff and Stephen Rawlins

Strategic Alternative

Figure 1 shows a technological strategy for developing a food production system that substantially increases carrying capacity and sustainability. Carrying capacity is increased by converting into human food a much larger fraction of the annual solar energy flux captured in the form of biomass. Sustainability is increased by use of perennial species that are more suited to the natural ecosystem, are less dependent on high inputs of fuel and chemicals from finite fossil fuel reserve, and [are] subject the soil to minimal erosion. . . .

Explication of Key Points

Primary plants grown in soil will be perennial, not annual. Limiting plant production in soil to perennial field crops grown primarily in rainfed geographic areas has several major benefits. Soil will suffer less

* Adapted from Marin H. Rogoff and Stephen L. Rawlins, "Food Security: A Technological Alternative," *Bioscience* 37(11), December 1987, pp. 800-808. Reprinted by permission of authors.

Figure 1: A Comparison of Traditional Food Production Technology and the Proposed Alternate Technology

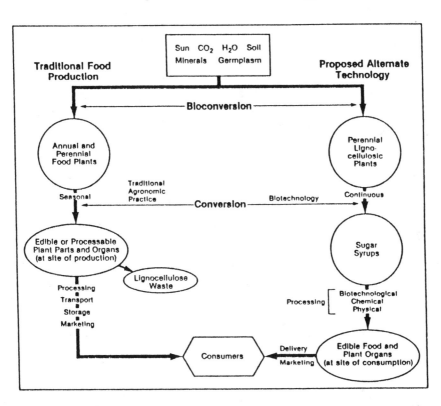

erosion, and both water and fossil energy will be spared by reducing the need for irrigation. With cellulosic materials as the major end product of soil-based agriculture, living perennials can serve as an easily stored reserve of feedstocks.

Because a reserve may contain a supply of feedstock that might last several years, long-term contingency planning is possible. Projected increases in food demand can be met simply by gradually expanding the area of this standing crop resource. In short, the annual yield of photosynthate can be stored, or harvested, as required. Noncrop cellulosic materials, previously useless as food other than through biotransformation by animals, become an emergency sump of reduced carbon for human food use. A hypothetical perennial hybrid with the attributes of tulip poplar, kenaf and a nitrogen-fixing symbiont can be envisioned as the field crop of choice.

Syrups will be the main commodity produced from soil-based agriculture. Processing of lignocellulose at the point of production allows by-products to be efficiently utilized. Practically everything, including the lignin, will either go into the conversion products or be used as fuel or fertilizer. "The farm" will be the primary point of food inventory control.

In the present system, food moves into long-distance transportation channels that may require refrigeration, cooling, controlled atmospheres or other measures to protect from spoilage. In the proposed system, only syrups will be transported to, and stored at, food production sites. The simplest means to move syrups is by pipeline. This low energy transport requires no special steps for preservation at usual syrup concentrations.

A demand-driven, year-round harvest mode would be possible. In our present food system, which is supply-driven, storage facilities must be large enough to carry the system from one harvest to the next. But in the proposed system, syrup storage facilities at the food production site would only need capacity to balance minor fluctuations in supply and demand. Year-round operations should significantly reduce the total size of unit processes, including storage facilities, thus reducing overall capital investment. There will be no off seasons.

Production of food at sites of consumption reduces inefficient unit operations inherent in the current system. The price of the food we now eat primarily reflects costs for labor, packaging, transportation, and storage. The cost of the food products at the farm gate often contributes only insignificantly to the overall price. Small incremental increases in unit process efficiency cannot reduce costs significantly for perishable products that must be stored for long periods of time. Costs for producing the basic food products in the proposed scenario may be greater than with the present system. But the processes that contribute most to present food costs should be drastically cut.

This scenario is compatible with the present demographic trend toward densely populated metropolitan areas linked by large suburban areas. As long as they conform to intensive land-use restrictions, high-intensity food production and processing facilities could be situated within or adjacent to megalopolitan complexes. The primary source of energy for these food production facilities would be natural sunlight captured on the farm and converted to a sugar syrup stream. Waste disposal at the food production sites should be minimal since only edible plant parts, not whole plants, would be produced there.

In addition to significantly reducing the current system's costs and problems, a spatially and temporally shortened marketing chain would reduce stored-product losses to pests. Also reduced or eliminated would be the cost for storage of raw food as mature or immature plant organs (e.g., seeds or seedbearing organs); long-term storage (e.g., freezing for raw or processed plant organs or parts); preservation processing (e.g., canning); packaging for long-term storage or long-distance transport; and processing of unripe harvested produce after transit or storage to ripen for market.

Food production in this alternative scenario is on-demand at demographically determined production sites in multipurpose facilities controlled by inventory-based systematics. Existing multipurpose, multisynthesis bioconversion or fermentation plants would seem to be reasonable models for these future systems.

Requiring only cellulose-rich plants for soil-based production, the technology would be less dependent on climatic factors than is the current system. Barring cataclysmic natural disaster on a continental scale (e.g., nuclear winter, global axis shifts, or total decertification), a sufficient supply of cellulose would be virtually assured. Even in extreme climates, perennial floras can flourish.

Although localized early or late freezes, intermittent dry spells or excessive rainfall may have disastrous effects on cropping systems whose products are annual plant organs or parts, their effects on perennial crops grown for lignocellulose should be reversible by a following favorable season. Shifts in production loci, aside from social impacts, will simply shorten or lengthen syrup supply lines. The alternate technology also has the potential of converting any cellulosic material to food, whether or not it was grown for the purpose.

Technical Basis

Space does not permit inclusion of the detailed emerging techniques in the physical and biological sciences that will make this alternative possible. Instead, this article identifies the nature of the technical changes required and the knowledge gaps that must be filled. This summary, then, is used as a basis for judging the probability that the projected technology can actually be developed.

There are three general technologies to be achieved. These technologies are (1) reduction of feedstocks to syrups, (2) production in vitro of major food components and (3) conversion of these components to aesthetically acceptable foods and production of edible plant organs or plant parts in artificial culture. . . .

[There follows a long section on the existing and needed R & D.]

Potential Constraints

Assuming that the technologies we have envisioned are technically feasible, what other factors might stand in the way of achieving a secure food supply with this scenario? Four potential constraints are readily apparent. These are biomass availability, energy dependency, processing and delivery costs, and consumer acceptability of high-tech food.

Biomass availability. The proposed scenario would reduce food production dependency on nonrenewable, resource-intensive agricultural practices. This proposal assumes that existing cellulose production capacity is adequate to generate the sugar feedstocks required. It is beyond this article's scope to determine preferred sites for biomass production under resource-conserving conditions. However, it is relatively simple to demonstrate that biomass availability will not be a constraint. . . . [A]lternate food production technologies would require only 2.8% conversion efficiency of unused lignocellulose, or 7% conversion efficiency for its cellulose, to provide all food consumed by the U.S. population.

Common sense, and knowledge of consumer demand for specific farm-produced products, dictate that soil-based agriculture will continue at some level. But, with current agricultural production providing over 30 times the necessary reduced carbon as waste, the acreage required for purposeful cellulose production is foreseen as relatively low. Conversion of only a small part of our highly productive agricultural land to the production of biomass would more than assure an adequate supply of food for the present population, leaving substantial arable reserve capacity for future population expansion. In short, the feedstocks required should be renewable as long as energy flow from the sun is sufficient to maintain the carbon cycle.

There is one additional point, pertinent to animal agriculture, related to the biomass issue. As in the case of soil-based agriculture, no total phase-out of animal production is expected. The proposed scenario will significantly reduce traditional cropping acreage, and so open up land not traditionally (or economically) available for animal production. A decrease in soil-based production of feed crops would be feasible with an opening of new range areas. Opening highly productive soils to range may also decrease the range area requirement per animal.

Energy dependency. No quantitative energy analysis can be made for processes that do not exist. But a general look at the energy budget of the current food system can indicate whether the new concepts provide any surprises that would negate the proposal's feasibility in terms of fossil fuel depletion.

The picture is not so bleak as that painted by Pimentel (1979) that, "The only means available to increase food production on limited arable land . . . will require greater inputs of energy for fertilizer and other crop production inputs." But it is abundantly clear that no one can convincingly argue that the existing food system can outlast our fossil fuel reserves. Our only hope for long-term survival is to develop a food system substantially less dependent on fossil fuels.

The proposed alterative food system is not radical in energy terms. It neither requires a new source of food energy nor a substitute for fossil fuel energy. It simply cycles through the human food chain a larger fraction of the annual carbon budget already being fixed in the leaves of growing plants. This strategy eliminates the need to pour even more fossil energy into intensive annual crop culture to meet the growing demand for food.

The food-chain fraction of fixed carbon can be increased by at least an order of magnitude. The fixed carbon now wasted is largely recycled through microbial decomposition of organic residues. Routing a larger fraction of it through the human food chain would greatly relieve the pressure on the food system and not perturb the balance of nature.

Even more important, the proposed scenario can reduce the currently high energy expenditure during food transfer and storage. The living reserve of standing perennial vegetation would cost little to maintain, and its potentially massive storage capacity would substantially raise the carrying capacity of the food system. It is the carrying capacity of the system that limits food security.

Economic feasibility. Traditional economic analysis is not very useful for long-term security issues, because no cost factors can be projected realistically 25-100 years. One way to look at future economic feasibility is by comparison with the current food cost distribution at the consumer level (Table 1). These unit costs are broadly divided into two operational categories: farm value and market bill. The latter represents the difference between payments to farmers for foodstuffs and consumer expenditures for these foods at food stores and eating places.

Table 1: Redistribution of Operating Expense Comparison: Current Versus Alternative Food Chain

Operational Element	Current Cost 1982 (¢)	Alternate Cost Projected (¢)	Net Gain (¢)	Projected Cost Rationale
Farm Value	28.0	4.0	+24.0	Assumes the costs of producing cellulose and converting it to sugar are the same as as those for sugarcane
Marketing Bill* Labor	32.0	10.0	+22.0	Automation and robotics
Packaging Materials	8.0	2.0	+6.0	Technology improvement, less storage-proofing
Intercity Transport	5.0	1.0	+4.0	Production at consumption site
Profit	4.5	4.5	0.0	No change unless nationalized
Cost of Selling/ Overhead**	22.5	22.5	0.0	No change unless nationalized
TOTAL	100.00	44.0	56.0	

*Determined for goods consumed both at home and outside.
**Includes repairs, interest, advertising, energy, rent and depreciation: 14¢; property taxes, insurance, accounting and professional services, promotion, bad debts and miscellaneous: 8.5¢.

It represented 72 cents of the consumer dollar in 1982 (US OTA 1983).

Reduced costs in the overall system could balance a sizable increase in costs now incurred beyond the farm gate. Even if biotechnological food processing costs were to double those in the present system, food cost to the consumer might not change.

What Table 1 does not point out is that future agriculture, whether [the] extension of existing technology to 100-acre controlled environment domes or the proposed alternate technology, will require a massive infusion of new capital. But new capital is scarce in the current food production, processing and distribution sectors. How to meet future capital demands must be a key issue in economic discussions. They should focus on return on investment, not primarily on operating costs of production, as they have in the past. In short, there is little sense in agonizing over economic feasibility of new technology, when future parameters will actually control the costs.

Consumer acceptability of new-technology foods. Future consumers are not expected to accept the next generation of ersatz coffee, or sawdust and algal bread. In the proposed scenario, plant parts grown in vitro would be held to the same quality standards as their current counterparts. Certain products, e.g., soft drinks or preserves, which now rely on artificial flavorings, are likely to be of better quality if prepared from plant tissues grown in vitro. We should detect no changes in our ketchup.

The challenge lies in developing technology to prepare high quality foods from singly produced food components. Today we include textured soy proteins in certain foods, but the vegetarian veal cutlet has never generated broad consumer demand. This failure is due in part to the fact that consumers who want meat do want meat, but there is also a quality factor involved.

The technical problems are not insurmountable. There is a great deal of research today attempting to define the basic determinants of food flavor and texture at the molecular level and to determine the biochemical pathways involved in their formation. This research includes animal- as well as plant-derived food products. For example, there is interest in overcoming the problem of "warmed-over flavor" in cooked beef, and "warmed-over texture" in pork. Single components of animal products should be no more difficult to produce biotechnologically than those from plant products. It is possible that culture of animal organs in vitro may require less time to attain than plant organs, since there is more basic knowledge of animal biochemistry and physiology than there is of plant biochemistry.

There is even research exploring the gustatory perception of smell. Success there could make an enormous contribution to the technology of fabricated foods.

Significant inroads can be made initially by the new technologies, as they emerge, in the preparation of the carbohydrate polymer foods.

One can readily visualize acceptable starchy foods—pastas, breads, sauces and various desserts. Dairy products would also appear a tempting target for these technologies.

There is no intent to stretch the technology's potential. But it appears that major dietary items can be replaced by items produced by the new technologies without sacrifice of quality. It is these major items, primarily carbohydrates, on which food security is based. The condiments are trivial.

5.

MUST A CHOICE BE MADE?

And there you have it—Chicken Little in the Flesh. Since there is "more basic knowledge of animal biochemistry and physiology than there is of plant biochemistry" (Rogoff and Rawlins, 1987), we may get biotechnologically produced animal organs even before we get vat-grown plant organs. In this efficient food system, "major dietary items"—a wide range of human foods—would not need to be grown, transported or stored at all. Only "trivial" condiments would need to be directly "finished" in the field. Much of what would be grown in the fields would be perennial plants that could serve as an emergency reserve. From these fields, only sugar syrups would be moved, probably by pipeline, and stored at food production sites. "Food" would be produced "on demand" at what the authors call "demographically determined production sites in multipurpose facilities controlled by inventory-based systematics," meaning, presumably, modern factories in cities.

As to what these on-demand foods would consist of, that is the genius of the proposal. Our only previous model is a substance called "soylent green" from the movie of the same name. In that nightmarish vision of the future, the planet has become so overpopulated that the elderly are coaxed into departure homes. There they are gently ushered into death so that their raw materials can be converted by biosynthesis into food. The alternative suggested by the present authors is indisputably more palatable "sourcewise," and its output also sounds much more promising.

If memory serves, the "soylent green" community could produce nothing more than a bland sort of fungus. Biotechnology has the potential for creating a much wider range of products. The technology for converting cellulosic materials to sugars is, the authors assert, almost here. The technologies for growing tomato or apple flesh from appropriate bacterial or tissue cultures are only a few steps beyond what is presently being done. (Perhaps less than that, given the present pace of biotechnology research. The GAO has reported an increase from 6,200 to 8,000 in *unexamined* biotechnology applications between January 1989 and mid-1990 [US GAO, 1990b]). Many of the tissues of interest are, in the words of Rogoff and Rawlins, "either embryos or . . . pericarp tissue (the fleshy, juicy tissues of the developed ovary)." The materials produced would be, for example, apple or tomato flesh— *natural,* not synthetic apple or tomato flesh.

Orange juice-producing vesicles are already being cultured in the laboratory, and although large-scale orange juice production by such a method is thought to be 15 to 20 years away, some observers consider such "bioprocess agriculture" inevitable (Anderson, 1990). Cotton fiber cells and cherry tissue have been cultured in the lab, and it is already possible to produce "natural" colors as well as "natural" vanilla and "natural" strawberry flavor without ever growing a vanilla bean or a strawberry plant. (Bock and Marsh, 1988; Dziezak, 1986; Ilker, 1987; Klausner, 1985; Pollack, 1987; Tisserat, et al, 1989; Vanilla: Is It the Real Thing?, 1987).

Giving microbes the capacity to produce the extracts of coffee, tea and cocoa (Pimentel, et al, 1989) now produced by trees and shrubs located in tropical countries would surely lessen processors' dependence on "remote parts of the world where . . . political instability . . . or the vagaries of weather" threaten the consistency of supply (Dziezak, 1986). To guess what our reduced dependence might mean to the "remote" countries themselves, one has only to consider the case of Madagascar and vanilla-free New Formula Coke. When Coca Cola introduced its new formula in 1985, the company consumed 30 percent of all the world's vanilla and Madagascar produced about three-fourths of the world's total vanilla supply. When U.S. consumers rejected the vanilla-free new formula in favor of "the real thing," the economy of Madagascar was saved (Vanilla . . . , 1985). A foretaste of its probable long-range fate is provided by the island of Negros in the Philippines where cane workers faced starvation when U.S. food processors turned to domestically produced corn syrup sweeteners in place of imported cane sugar (Stalker, 1990). One could argue that in the long run, lessened dependence on unreliable first world markets, fewer cocoa, coffee and tea plantations, and more production for local consumption will be the Third World's salvation. In the short term, the sudden cut off of export earnings would be devastating (Busch, et al, 1991).

Model or Warning?

Despite the technological conviction behind the Rogoff and Rawlins scenario, there is no reason to fear that someone in the 1990s will eat the last pizza sauced with vine-grown tomatoes, or that the apple orchards not yet replaced by housing developments will necessarily be torn out *because we have learned to make applesauce in the lab.* If developing countries' coffee, tea and cocoa crops were rendered worthless by our laboratory extracts, it would be wild speculation to imagine that these countries might become our sole source of fresh produce because their cheap labor would make it profitable for them to grow whole plants just to bring their ovaries to maturity. And a United States that provided no market at all for fresh produce seems beyond imagining— a United States population grown so accustomed to foods of uncertain origin that it would settle for foods factory-"grown" from "natural" materials, believing that science had at last conquered nature. Such scenarios are only speculation; yet to walk down the aisle of a present-day supermarket, wondering what our great grandparents would have thought of it all, is to realize that drastic change in the direction of greater artifice is not a fantasy in the U.S., but the present norm.

Furthermore, it is quite irrelevant to the questions being raised in this essay whether any of these particular scenarios come true. The major triumphs of biotech may prove to be herbicide-resistant grain crops, more milk from fewer cows and field-grown, shelf-stable tomatoes (Fisher, 1990). The idea that a rational solution to our food supply problems is to grow cheap raw materials in distant fields and construct foods in the cities has produced much of the present glitzy food supply; the scenario proposed is different only in degree. That biotechnology may make possible an even more "unnatural" approach to food production does not mean that a system such as Rogoff and Rawlins proposes will inevitably or even likely replace the system we presently have.

What is important about the Rogoff and Rawlins scenario, therefore, is the fact that it represents one end point of a particular philosophy, although I have serious doubts about it ever coming true. To a system already driven by the simplest economic definition of "efficiency" and an illusory control over nature achieved at great energy cost, it promises more efficiency and even greater control over nature, which it offers to deliver for a *lesser* input of energy. Indeed, this system dispenses with nature altogether for a good part of the food production process, making use only of the capacity of plants under "natural" conditions to fix solar energy, but not of their capacity to produce foods humans enjoy.

Moreover, however alien the production system this scenario promises, it does seem to offer a solution to many of the soil erosion, ground water overuse and pesticide pollution problems that some observers have been looking to low-input sustainable agriculture to solve. What may be equally important is that it solves them in a way that does nothing to interfere with the increasing concentration of control in the food industry, which is why there will be pressure to move in the direction it implies.

Making a Choice of Futures

Now some people may view this scenario as so obviously absurd as to require no comment, while others may view it as so attractive an extension of our control over nature as to require no rebuttal. I subscribe to neither of these views.

The Rogoff and Rawlins' scenario is deeply disturbing because it so clearly reveals that there is not a single obvious (and inevitable) solution to the problems besetting our industrial agriculture. Contrary to the assumptions of those who hope that the public's fear of pesticide residues—of "unnaturalness" in all its guises—will drive the system toward the sort of soft-path agriculture earlier described as sustainable, the Rogoff and Rawlins' scenario makes it clear that there is more than one way to skin a cat. *In order to get chemically pure food, we would not need to have what we think of as agriculture at all.* Those vat-grown food materials would be as *pesticide-free* as the produce now being sold in California supermarkets. And if the FDA would go along with it, they could even be billed as "natural" (Make Everything 'Natural'..., 1990). After all, beer brewing and cheese making are being presented in food technology journals as part of the 8,000-year-old tradition of biotechnology (Knorr and Sinskey, 1985; Knorr, 1987). If the buying public's criterion for a successful food-producing system is merely that it should be able to serve up produce free of undesirable residues and capable of being labeled "natural," then buying into the system that Rogoff and Rawlins advocate can undoubtedly solve that problem long before we reach Chicken Little. If what we want is simply biologically produced, pesticide-free food, we seem to have a choice. We can vote for a Sane-Humane-Ecological (SHE) system that works with nature or a Hyper-Expansionist (HE) system that further increases our hegemony over the biosphere.

The final chapter of this volume will look at some possibilities for pushing the food system in what I view as the right direction. Before we get there, however, two other issues need to be examined. In the remainder of this chapter, we will consider various objections that might be raised—by those who believe the Chicken Little scenario is either inevitable or inevitably doomed—to the notion that making a choice is necessary. Chapter 6 will then examine the reasons why a Chicken Little future seems not only undesirable, but dangerous.

No One Is in Charge?

Among the objections that might be raised to the notion that we must (or *can*) actively oppose visions like that of Rogoff and Rawlins, there is the obvious one that opposition is both fruitless and unnecessary because no one is actually in charge of what happens in the food system; therefore, its future is inevitable. You cannot stop science (read *technology*), so the argument goes, and since science (read *technology*) is pushing the system, responding as if someone were in charge is paranoid and imputes human agency to what is the natural course of events. Brewster Kneen, in a recent issue of his food system newsletter, *The Ram's Horn,* notes that there is a lot of this assumption-of-inevitability writing in official future-of-agriculture documents. Commenting on a report from Agriculture Canada entitled "Growing Together—A Vision for Canada's Agri-food Industry," he finds language designed to "mystify, alienate and fatalize." The report, he notes, is full of the passive voice, full of references to agriculture *evolving,* or of the need for everyone to adapt to the changing "agrifood system" (Kneen, 1989). The underlying assumption in such forecasts is that we are all in this together, Cargill, Philip Morris, the ad agencies, the farmer forced off his land by bankruptcy, the bank that forces him and consumers like you and me. The inference is that the agrifood industry is as much a victim of the inevitable march of progress as anyone else.

Which is, of course, nonsense. As the largest industry in the United States, the agrifood industry is very powerful indeed, as anyone who has attempted to reason with it knows. All those who have worked to structure policies that would help farmers continue to grow food and help consumers make rational food choices are frighteningly aware of the forces arrayed against even the contemplation of a change in direction, and of the hostility and contempt directed toward groups that try to generate citizen resistance to present trends.

The Rogoff and Rawlins scenario would inevitably concentrate control over the food system into even fewer hands (a sobering idea given that our largest food corporation is now Philip Morris, a producer of Marlboros with a lack of interest in our health requiring no elaboration). Even greater concentration of control seems much more plausible—unless it is consciously opposed—than does any scenario that envisions decentralization for the sake of environmental and social good. If we are to change direction in the food system, it will have to be by intentionally combatting the forces that—in gaining control over every aspect of the food system, from seed to table—mold the choices offered us.

What makes the Chicken Little scenario useful, therefore, is that it requires us to ask ourselves how far we will permit the system to be moved toward artifice and monopoly before we set out seriously to fight back. It requires us to assess our mutual ability to respond wisely to proffered "technological solutions"—in the food supply and elsewhere.

The system is being *moved,* not simply trending whither it will. Someone is sure to point out, however, that although industry may strive to lead our tastes, 90 percent of new products fail. Perhaps the consumer still is in charge and will reject foods grown in vats from sugar syrups. When I first heard about Rogoff and Rawlins' scenario, I mentioned it to Wes Jackson whose Land Institute in Salina, Kansas, has long devoted itself to developing a perennial polyculture that could—planted on former prairie land that should never have been broken to the plough—overcome the unsustainable erosion that now afflicts that region. I pointed out to Wes that his planned perennial crop might be ideal for conversion into sugar syrups in this new scenario. What did he think we ought to do about that? I knew the scenario would be as appalling to him as it had been to me and other land-attached people, but his response surprised me. "Consumers would never accept such foods," was what he said. "Most of them wouldn't know the difference," was my reply.

Counting on Consumers?

Do eaters of the $1.5 billion worth of frozen pizzas sold every year know where the tomato sauce on their pies comes from? Would most of those people know—or care—if it came from a vat in Rahway, New Jersey? After all, Rogoff and Rawlins assure us, consumers will detect no changes in their ketchup; and soft drinks prepared with biotechnologically produced "natural" flavors may be better than the ones we get now (see Chapter 4, page 49). The Campbell Soup Company is predicting that "25 percent of all cars will have microwave ovens" by the year 2000 (Hamel, 1989). Consumers who will buy (and defend their purchase of) flagrantly wasteful and expensive microwave popcorn or frozen microwavable soup and sandwich combinations (to eat in their cars!) cannot be counted on to save the food system from its excesses.

All right, you may argue. But you are talking about *processed* food. Vat-grown applesauce surely won't satisfy people's growing interest in, and appetite for, fresh fruits and vegetables. One must be careful not to confuse visibility with popularity. Some years ago, in a book entitled, *A Sense of Place: The Artist and the American Land,* my husband showed how artists from the 16th century onward had responded to the abundance of the American land. "Nineteenth century painters went out into the wilderness to bring back reports about a land we did not know," he wrote in the introduction. "Painters now report about a land we risk forgetting" (Gussow, 1972). That passage was brought to mind by the astonishing proliferation of gorgeous pictures of gorgeous produce that now decorates calendars, date books, cookbooks, notebook covers and the like. Of course, the produce sections are growing larger in many supermarkets, but much of the growth to date seems to derive from the same search for novelty that drives the market for microwavable single-serving portions or clever crackers (Gussow, 1985). Yet even at the height of what seems like a wave of interest in produce, government figures show that fresh fruit consumption may actually be declining among some groups of consumers (Rizek, 1989), and 49 percent of Americans consume no "garden" vegetable at all on a given day— canned, frozen *or* fresh (Patterson and Block, 1988). So clearly everyone is not paying attention. Of course, some consumer segments will want exotic produce just as they do now; they will doubtless be able to fly it in from poor countries overseas just as they do now, merely accelerating our growing dependence on imported produce.

Oh, yes, you say, but things are changing. Americans' concerns about health, especially about cancer, will lead them inevitably to fresh fruits and vegetables as the repositories of those new disease fighting chemicals. What such a hope fails to acknowledge is that our reductionist science and our extractive technologies have been profiting from food for years by the simple expedient of removing wanted parts from wholes and selling the parts back to consumers at a higher price. The oat bran rage was merely a late manifestation of this familiar phenomenon. The management teams driving the food industry do not see much long-term profit in fresh produce simply because of its natural variability (uniformity is the industrial goal), its natural tendency to decay and the vulnerability of its supply to uncontrollable climatic and other forces.

The denaturing approach to profiting from "food" was long ago laid out in advice offered to the food processing industry by the Arthur D. Little Company. At a time when global food shortages threatened to drive raw materials prices up, they suggested the processors could decrease their vulnerability to nature by developing the sorts of complex food products that offered "much greater latitude in the raw material selection process." Little pointed out that standard low-value food items or commodity-like products make the processor vulnerable because they "are not easily reformulated without loss of identity." However, "the further a product's identity moves from a specific raw material—that is, the more processing steps involved—the less vulnerable its processor" (Little, 1974).

Grocery shelves are now filled with products based on that recipe for success; it would be foolish, therefore, to ignore some more recent Arthur D. Little advice to the food processing industry suggesting that products at the "food-drug interface" may be a new growth area (Companies Can Capitalize . . . , 1988). Even now the National Cancer Institute is engaged in a multimillion dollar program that may result in formulated food products enriched with what are presumed to be protective levels of phytochemicals (NCI to Spend $51 Million . . . , 1989). At the Biotech USA conference held late in 1990, there was talk of "molecular pharming" (Use of Plants . . . , 1990), and the year 1991 opened with the first "Nutraceuticals and Pharmafoods" conference, which promised to help participants cope with the regulatory barriers to marketing "medical foods," "orphan foods," "designer foods" and "healthy foods" (Nutraceuticals . . ., 1990). The sorts of pro-active health claims such foods would be able to make are what the editor of *New Product News* called "the hottest food-selling tool today." What

"The most significant food science innovation of the last fifty years" isn't even food.

This week many people are receiving awards for contributing to society through invention and discovery. And recently, aseptic packaging –the drink box–also garnered special recognition. The Institute of Food Technologists, a professional scientific society devoted to developments that improve the world's food supply, has cited aseptic packaging for its advancements and positive effect on the quality of our lives.

This packaging has been named "the most significant food science innovation of the last 50 years" based on breakthroughs in food safety and nutrition. That's because drink box technology, unlike conventional packaging, makes it possible to maintain the nutrient content and flavor of beverages while still ensuring purity. So while drink boxes are not an innovative new food per se, their innovation does provide tastier, healthier, more nutritious food choices.

The makers of the DRINK BOX

[No Comment!]

they have in mind are things like "orange juice with the phytochemical content of 20 oranges or salt- and fat-free beef stroganoff with high concentrations of allium" (O'Neill, 1990). The *New York Times'* story reporting on these new developments did include a recipe for a homemade "Oncophobic Onion Soup," but it took two hours and 40 minutes to make from raw vegetables and dry beans. Why bother? If chemicals that replicate broccoli's reputed virtues as a cancer preventative can be added to a formulated meal made irresistibly tasty and microwavable, then even the fear of dying cannot be counted on to save agriculture.

Many years ago, a writer named Jean Carper wrote a column for *Newsweek* in which she suggested that all of us might end up eating foods made of nothing but additives because they, at least, could be tested for safety. We were so polluting the food-producing environment, she argued, that such fabricated foods would be safer than field-grown ones. Recently Carper wrote a book called *The Food Pharmacy,* discussing the medicinal use of various whole foods (Carper, 1988). Too late, it seems. The food industry has taken her at her (earlier) word and is doing it with "natural" chemicals.

Nutritionists are seldom asked at parties anymore about whole wheat bread; they are often asked about Omega-3-fatty acids, calcium, selenium and Beta-carotene. In the name of commerce, as we have noted earlier, foods are increasingly being fragmented and served up as pieces—or as entirely novel "restructured" pure foods. Some time ago, *Prepared Foods* cheerfully announced that "the era of artificial foods seems to have arrived, and for products like shrimp, olives and black currants, it's becoming difficult to distinguish the man-made item from the real thing" (Lund, 1987).

In the ongoing war between the real and the artificial, it is surely bad news for nature that the Giant and Safeway food stores in the nation's capital closed their special organic produce sections at the beginning of 1990 because of what they said was a lack of public interest (Sugarman, 1990). At its present level of sophistication about food production, the buying public may not be counted on to block the introduction of Chicken Little, breaded and fried, or even—somewhat more healthfully—mesquite grilled.

Counting the (Money) Costs

Admittedly, the economics of the Chicken Little scenario seem at the moment a more serious barrier. Tissue culture-based manufacturing plants are currently incapable (so far as we know) of producing tomato sauce cheap enough to use on a pizza, and Chicken Little McNuggets would need to compete pricewise with the flesh from bargain basement battery chickens. We know from past experience, however, that technological solutions that promise to free us from naturally imposed limits have a great impetus behind them and sometimes develop even when they do not seem economically rational—especially if they further concentrate power in the hands of those who already possess it. (Nuclear energy, for example, has always had to be subsidized by cheap fossil fuel energy, but that did not stop governments from pursuing its promise of "cheap, unlimited power.")

Indeed, the promised ultimate "cheapness" of this new industrial food is certain to be cited as one of the arguments in its favor. Humanitarians ought not to stand in the way of these biotechnological advances, we will be told, since *ultimately* these processes will produce food "even cheaper" than that we now enjoy, cheap enough even for the poor. (The corollary argument that food produced by organic/sustainable methods will inevitably be more expensive remains unproven, but is often trotted out to ridicule as selfish "Yuppies" those who espouse such methods.)

That there are countries much poorer than our own, where even the poor can afford to eat, and that there are hungry people in the U.S. now (despite this nation's cheap raw materials policy) ought to be answer enough to the argument that "progress" must be allowed to make our food even cheaper. Moreover, on a global scale, it is evident that urging peasants to grow inedible raw materials that will be turned into "food" only when they reach the cities is a recipe for even more widespread rural starvation than exists presently, when the foods the peasants grow are merely siphoned off for sale to the rich. Those who have money can eat now. Those who don't, can't—and won't—however clever our food becomes, *unless* human society becomes more humane.

Can technical safety objections be counted on to block the road to such a drastically altered food system as the Rogoff and Rawlins scenario describes? Will our Food and Drug regulators balk at the monumental task of developing adequate safety tests for the products of such processes and thereby manage to delay the introduction of these new "natural" foods? One need not be a pessimist to conclude that our regulatory agencies are not up to such a challenge. As Chapter 1 made clear, our food safety apparatus has scarcely begun to acknowledge publicly its inability to certify the harmlessness of the multitudinous changes "progress" has already introduced into our foods, and these are derived, for the most part, from familiar field-grown materials. This system cannot be counted on either to certify the safety of, or to block the introduction of the further novelty biotechnology will introduce (Schneider, 1990c).

There are, in short, no evident barriers—other than technical ones that can surely be overcome—standing in the way of a system that could produce Chicken Little. Whether or not we find the Rogoff and Rawlins scenario—either in whole or in part—unpalatable, there is a choice to be made. The next chapter reflects on some of the reasons why the "right" choice seems to be the one that leads away from "Chicken Little."

6.

DO WE NEED TO PRODUCE
MORE FOOD?

Those who have followed the argument to this point may have noted my failure to mention a motive that purports to be driving the development of such scenarios as that of Rogoff and Rawlins—the impending global shortages of food. A major reason agribusiness gives for its own determined pursuit of biotechnology is that only this new technique will allow producers to meet the world's food demands into the next century (Schneider, 1990a).

On the face of it such an argument seems compelling. It is obvious that on various parts of the globe various groups of humans have been pushing nature to the hilt, seemingly to produce more food. Here in the U.S., as noted earlier, farmers are using irreplaceable ground water to grow fodder for livestock, investing heavily in nitrogen fertilizers, insecticides and herbicides (and the machinery to apply them), as well as row planting the best agricultural land year after year (despite destructive levels of soil erosion) in order to boost production to the limit. Windbreaking hedgerows planted after the dustbowl of the 1930s were long ago ripped up and fields planted fence to fence.

Similar efforts to coax more food from the earth have been going on even more desperately around the world. Everywhere the poor and their grazing animals extract the last of the fertility from some of the planet's most vulnerable soils, turning flat lands into deserts, hillsides into bare rock. An outsider looking casually down on the planet might reasonably conclude that the human species is indeed pushing nature to her limits and beyond in a desperate effort to produce enough food for an exponentially growing population.

The global food policy argument that emerged in the 1960s and 1970s seemed to reflect some such conclusion: Humankind was reaching the earth's food production limits, so this argument went. Was it sensible for industrial countries to "prop up" nations that could not (or *would not* through agricultural modernization) feed themselves? Was it even humanitarian to provide food to people who would not, or could not, cut their birthrates? Was food aid merely giving encouragement to "slovenly rulers" whose subjects would inevitably turn more food into more babies?

The apparently simple construct that emerged from this analysis was that, given too many people and too little food, choices of whom to feed would have to be made. One suggestion—that aid ought not to be given to countries in which "the population growth trend has already passed the agricultural potential" (Paddock and Paddock, 1976)—mercilessly revealed the flaws in the analysis. Universally applied, such a standard would have abandoned the U.K., Japan and Israel, the populations of which had long ago passed the potential of their existing agricultural systems. Thus was clarified the fact that it was not the ability to *grow* food that was the criterion of salvageability but the ability to *pay* for it (Gussow, 1978).

The U.S., with its abundant natural resources, posed the population/food question to itself in terms of generosity, priding itself on its largesses, confounding its enemies with Food for Peace. Only later did it become evident that bargain American grain had often been used to create animal feeding industries in countries hard pressed to sustain them at market prices. Americans had thoughtfully used their food prowess—as a contemporary Secretary of Agriculture so candidly put it—as a tool. Not really food for peace, but rather food to rivet alliances (Block to Serve. . . , 1981).

By the mid-1970s, public thinking (by that small part of the public concerned at all about who goes hungry and why) had begun to be affected by a modest but influential text first published in 1971—Frances Moore Lappé's best-selling *Diet for a Small Planet* (Lappé, 1971). It was Ms. Lappé's argument that the limits of global food-producing capacity had not nearly been approached. Indeed, the U.S. had so much surplus grain that it was poured down the gullets of meat animals to fatten them for slaughter. So the world hunger concern generated in the mid-1970s was translated in some quarters into a recommendation to eat one less hamburger apiece and send the money saved to CARE.

As the decade advanced, a series of new, more radical analyses began to emerge: the poor could not afford to buy food unless they had work; giving them food only made them more dependent; and—most startling of all—the poor and hungry could feed themselves if only they had access to resources of land, seeds, water and credit. They lacked such access, hunger activists argued, because of the entrenched powers of local aristocracies and the growing power of transnational corporations. The latter made their profits utilizing the soils and labor of the poor to produce luxuries for the rich, even as they profited from transporting the grain surpluses of the wealthy back to the poor. Some argued that all food aid was ultimately destructive, since in one way or another it supported the powerful, thereby thwarting revolutions that might—these critics hoped—give the poor control over their own food-producing resources. (See, for example, George, 1977; Lappé and Collins, 1977; Perelmen, 1977; Tudge, 1977; Dahlberg, 1979.)

The 1980s gave another turn to the screw. At the rich world's urging, the poor world had borrowed heavily, most often for the kinds of "development" projects favored by the lenders—including such amenities as roads to the world's coastlines over which the debtors could more easily export their natural wealth. By the mid 1980s, despite inflows of "foreign aid" from the developed world, poor nations were paying out to the rich ones $50 *billion* a year *more* than they were taking in from all sources (Taylor, 1990). By 1988, the total Third World debt amounted to more than one *trillion* dollars and interest payments alone were exhausting national treasuries. To fail to try to pay was to fall out of the international economic system. As the poor world sold what it could, countries that were once "developing" fell further and further behind. Croplands, mines and forests were exploited to produce not goods the poor themselves could use or eat, but foods and other products they could sell to make their interest payments (Watkins, 1986; Schatan, 1987; George, 1990). Since debtors would accept only "hard" currencies, the poor couldn't even sell to each other; they had to sell to the already rich. In the mid 1980s, the food-rich U.S. found itself importing food from some of the poorest countries in the world.

Why Overproduce?

This bit of history is intended to place in some sort of context several relevant facts. First, at the moment there is plenty of food in the world for everyone. If food—or the resources to grow it—were not so maldistributed, there would be enough for everyone to eat now, even with the present high level of meat consumption.* A second relevant fact is that although U.S. farmers have been pushing their land to the limits of its productive capacity for many years, it is evident that nature is not in this case being flogged so she can outrun famine. The heedless extraction of irreplaceable ground water, the costly drain of topsoil down major waterways, the energy-expensive nitrogen fixes with which U.S. farmers have sought to boost soil fertility, the chemical warfare they have waged to defend their crops against pests (many of them generated by chemicals applied to formerly harmless weeds and insects)—these were not yearly sacrifices of sustainability reluctantly abandoned in the face of rising hunger.

This leads to the third relevant fact, namely, that these approaches to food production which have been promoted in the name of ending hunger cannot over time feed growing numbers of people simply because they are too destructive to the underlying resource base. To begin with, it is undemonstrated that the production systems with which traditional ones were replaced are really more productive if costs now externalized are all counted in. As the analysis in Chapter 2 showed, unlimited energy and abundant high-quality land have fueled the enviable successes of U.S. industrial farming. Around the world, as in the United States, farmers are *mining* their soils and their groundwaters, thereby *under*mining their future. And destruction elsewhere is often much more advanced than it is here since those who are most stressing their lands seldom began with soils as rich or fossil energy as abundant.

The myth that the U.S. has spent its own soils, and is now plunging forward into biotechnology principally to save others from starvation, obscures the faiths and fears that actually drive the system toward the likes of Chicken Little. Faith in the profit motive as a regulator of distribution is clearly overriding, as earlier chapters have suggested. But fear of losing control over nature—and an inflated view of humanity's ability to effectively get control of nature—is another motivating force. The urgency of profit as a shaper of the food system has been exhaustively explored elsewhere (George, 1977; Kramer, 1977; Perelmen, 1977; Tudge, 1977; Morgan, 1979), but it would be

---

* We will, of course, ultimately run out of production capacity if world population continues to increase. But, as the recent experience of China shows, it is not simply more food, but a fairer distribution of resources and the chance for a better life that induces people to *want* fewer children.

misleading to conclude that it is only lust for profit that pushes the food system toward Chicken Little. The system is also being driven by the conviction that the only *rational* approach is one that brings under corporate control as much as possible of the natural world.

To a certain extent, of course, the increasing tendency of agribusiness to control everything from research to restaurants can be interpreted merely as another way of reducing the risk of unprofitability by bringing supply and demand along much of the food chain under one corporate umbrella. But taking the profit motive for granted will allow for a fuller exploration of the need for *control* as a motive, which on its own explains a good deal about a food production system that appears to be in the process of destroying its own resource base. In their search for total control, giant food companies express a profound but common misunderstanding that colors the entire relationship between an increasingly urbanized humanity and the natural world, namely, the belief that it is *necessary* (and possible) for humans to control nature.

Any discussion of why the industrial lust for control over nature is misguided must begin by acknowledging a point of view that is considered in most scientific circles as beneath serious consideration—the "deep ecology" viewpoint. People who call themselves deep ecologists hold that the human species—one among multitudes—must on moral grounds stop behaving as if it were entitled to use all the others for any purpose it chooses (Naess, 1988). A "living" headless chicken, a deep ecologist would argue, is simply *wrong,* as is the drugged, debeaked battery chicken or the Thanksgiving turkey "built" with such a heavy breast that it can barely hold itself erect. The argument that it is wrong to use animals any way we choose becomes increasingly compelling as our species' capacity for manipulation enlarges. More than "bleeding hearts" would surely shrink from the unconscious cruelty of a scientist commenting to the *Washington Times* about the suffering of a pig crippled by genetic manipulation. "We're at the Wright Brothers' stage compared to the 747. We're (sic!) going to crash and burn for a number of years" (Singer, 1990). It was more difficult to object to a well-kept flock of free-range chickens than it is to see the evil (to use a flagrantly unscientific word) in a row of headless Chicken Littles, even though the intent behind each of these production facilities—to provide chicken meat to the human species—may be the same.

While I respect the deep ecology viewpoint, and find myself drawn ever closer to it as time goes by, it has been eloquently argued elsewhere (Singer, 1990) and is neither the only, nor necessarily the most convincing, argument against running headlong down the road that leads to

Chicken Little. Moreover, it is an argument likely to "turn off" some of those who might otherwise be inclined to agree that any scenario leading to the takeover of nature by corporate biotechnology is deeply frightening on a number of grounds.

Chief among the things that ought to be alarming about such a potential coup is the demonstrated inability of humans to manage large and complex systems without occasional life-threatening catastrophes. Rogoff and Rawlins offer to reduce the cost in energy and human labor in taking control of a multitude of variables. The end result is not a food chain in which nature with the help of farmers ultimately controls the year's supply of apples—with human harvesters and truckers controlling their picking and movement, and human integrity and care protecting their freshness on the lengthening path from farmer to consumer. The end result is a food chain in which no serious attention need be given to what is grown or transported, since the first is a hardy cellulosic stock and the second is simple sugars derived from it. Nor need society concern itself much with the growers or transporters. Once converted into sugars, the fate of what will come to be "food" will depend not on the vagaries of weather or the reliability of truckers unions, but on the structural integrity of a system of pipelines and on the infallibility of the computers that control the facility where the pipelines end.

Such a system seems on the face of it to offer an attractive reduction of complexity; its apparent simplicity seems to provide a kind of security against accident that the other system, the one dependent on nature and other humans, does not possess. In that sense the Chicken Little scenario is just one more step in the process whereby Western man (and increasingly Western woman as well) attempts to provide for himself a greater measure of well-being and security by overpowering nature and eliminating the input of other humans. Nature is seen in this scenario as a hostile adversary in need of control: humans are viewed as expensive and unreliable.

Nature as Adversary

To begin with nature, I came across a truly exquisite expression of this nature-as-enemy attitude in a book put out by FAO entitled *Traditional and Non-Traditional Foods* (Ferrando, 1981). The author begins by addressing that straw man issue to which nutritionists give so much angry attention: "What is a natural food?" He goes on: "It is very difficult to answer this question. The people who propagandize or seek out such foods would themselves be hard put to answer it." And then, no longer interested in speculating on what a natural food might be, the author is abruptly concerned that his readers should understand nature's hostility: "Everything that corresponds to the usual order of nature or reflects nature or that has been constrained by nature is not necessarily good. ... The manifestations of nature are many and varied and agricultural products are but one form. Nature is not good per se. At best, it is indifferent to man; otherwise, it is downright hostile. Man has been able to exist on the face of the earth because he has been able to acquire the knowledge needed to thwart this hostility, to increase nature's margin of tolerance and, *sometimes, albeit rarely, to harmonize its needs with his for a while"* (Ferrando, 1981; emphasis added).

What on earth does this mean? Does the author really intend to say that humans can only occasionally pay attention to nature's "needs?" Doesn't he know that nature is still in charge and that any illusions to the contrary are guaranteeably temporary? Planet earth would soon be entirely uninhabitable if nature (whether "it," "he" or "she") decided to stop providing what Paul Ehrlich called "free" services—"maintenance of the gaseous quality of the atmosphere, amelioration of climate, operation of the hydrologic cycle (including the control of floods and the provision of fresh water to agriculture, industry and homes) disposal of wastes, recycling of the nutrients essential to agriculture and forestry, generation of soils, pollination of crops, provision of food from the sea, and maintenance of a vast genetic library from which humanity has already drawn the very basis of its civilization" (Ehrlich, 1989).

But the notion that nature is not to be trusted is widespread and takes increasingly curious forms as we "civilized" people move ever more deeply into our constructed world. Noting that U.S. consumers ingest 283,106 tons of flavor chemicals a year in unprocessed foods, the author of a recent article defending the use of added flavors asks: "Is it not safer to consume a product that has 20 or less well-defined and safety-tested flavor chemicals than one that has hundreds of [nature's] chemicals of questionable safety or known toxicity?" (Reiniccius, 1989). The safest food supply, in short, would be one created exclusively by food chemists.

Such "man-knows-best" attitudes are widespread among scientists, technologists and ordinary U.S. citizens, who have been weaned on tales of science magically transforming their lives. Helped along by the undoubted achievements of Western science and its attendant technologies in bringing nature's gifts under human control, modern Americans are bedazzled by what are billed as "scientific" solutions to their problems. The cause for concern here is not that scientific knowledge is limited, that it cannot deal with values, purposes, meanings or "quality." The worry is that those who are non-scientists tend to overestimate the extent to which science really comprehends even the concrete relationships it claims to be best at comprehending. Non-scientists misunderstand how small a distance science has gone in grasping the world and how little, therefore, it can be counted on to keep everything under control.

This confusion is helped along by scientists themselves. Psychologist Philip Slater has observed that science can only function at all by believing "that fundamentally it's on top of things—that it has a firm conceptual grip on the universe with only a few bugs to iron out," although "any really intelligent scientist knows how preposterous this assumption is." The only alternative seems to be to give a hearing to every crazy idea that comes along about how things work—an alternative that would prevent scientists from functioning at all (Slater, 1977).

Although the operating illusion that they have things under control may be necessary to the functioning of some scientists, the public's acceptance of that illusion is increasingly dangerous to the functioning of the biosphere. The reason is very simple. The biosphere has (at least until now) maintained *itself;* to the extent that non-scientists are deluded about who is actually in charge, they risk allowing the destruction of the complex interrelated and little-understood (perhaps, even less understandable) systems upon which the integrity of our species depends for survival.

A practitioner of ecology—the scientific discipline that looks at these systems—has pointed out that there are only three things of importance his profession can offer to decision makers. These are "specific predictions on certain limited problems, a description of human dependence on the public service functions of the ecological systems, [and] the lesson that humanity should be extremely conservative in its treatment of earth's ecosystems." While ecological science, he goes on, cannot at the moment accurately predict "the consequences of any given act of extinction, it can predict with extreme accuracy the end result of continuing our assaults on Earth's systems: the collapse of civilization as we know it" (Ehrlich, 1981).

Since comprehension of these sustaining systems is so limited, it seems a potentially suicidal act of faith in human wit and nature's continued good will to propose the takeover through biotechnology of even the planet's evolution—an act which some of those most equipped to know view as despairingly risky. Even before genetic engineering was selling stocks, the new discipline was heralded as opening up "the prospect of the final conquest [sic!] of [the] food supply" (Brooks, 1971). Biologist Robert Sinsheimer has argued, rather, that humanity risks destroying the "delicately balanced intricate and self-sustaining network" that supports, among other things, food production. "Do we want increasingly to engineer the planet," he has asked, "so that its continued functioning requires the continuous input of human intelligence? Do we want to convert the planet into a huge Skylab?" (Sinsheimer, 1981).

Magic or Science?

It is hard to know whether the problem-solving claims made on behalf of each new technology that comes down the pike—such as "this will *really* conquer world hunger"—are simply rationalizations for joining what Schumacher called "the forward stampede," or whether scientists and their attendant technicians actually lose sight of their own limits. Some observations by anthropologist Laura Nader suggest the latter. Reflecting on her experiences on a National Academy of Sciences "energy futures" committee, Nader came to the conclusion that the physical scientists on that panel behaved less wisely than the "primitive" Trobriand Island fishermen studied almost four decades earlier by anthropologist Bronislaw Malinowski.

Trobriand Islanders, Malinowski found, were like people from all cultures—operating in both profane and sacred domains. On the one hand, they had science; on the other, they had magic and religion. They made use of each when appropriate occasions arose and fully recognized which one they were using at any given time. When they fished in familiar inner lagoons, they used a body of scientific knowledge derived from long observation of the behavior of nature and their own boats. But, when they had to take their small craft into the less predictable open seas, they recognized that their science was insufficient, and that they could no longer protect themselves by relying on their own knowledge and skills. On such occasions they sought safety in magic. In hunting food, in other words, the Trobriand Islanders sometimes used science and sometimes used magic *and were careful to distinguish between the two* (Nader, 1981).

Nader concluded that the scientists and technologists she observed did not recognize when they were using science and when they were using magic, thereby risking not merely a few fishing boats but all of human civilization. Applied more widely to the scientific enterprise, her conclusion seems inescapable. Science demonstrates that civilization's effluents are threatening the climate, the ozone layer, the purity of the ground water, the productivity of the oceans. Only magic can assure us that these threats will surely be resolved. Yet as events begin to suggest that industrial activities threaten human life-support systems, officialdom calls in scientists to assure its citizens that there is no choice but to run even faster. Only tomorrow's science and the technologies it allows, they assert, can resolve whatever threats today's science and technology have produced. So when science reports that it may be feasible to create plant and animal parts in systems torn out of nature and moved to the pipeline and the giant retort, the assurance comes that more science can solve whatever problems these new technologies create. But only magic can guarantee that science will be capable of rescuing humans from their own audacity.

Restrained Nature, Unrestrained Humanity

Like DDT, DES, EDTA and the rest of the designer chemicals that consumers now unwittingly ingest, designer genes will enter the human food chain well before those who promote them understand any of their long-term implications. This newest toy comes with the standard guarantee—that humanity can choose to use it exclusively for The Good of Humanity. Of course, most of "humanity" has no vote. Moreover, those who have tried to vote "no" have been told that "you can't stop progress." And those very folks who thus have found themselves powerless to prevent untested technologies from being rapidly introduced are supposed to be reassured by the claim that they *will* have the power to prevent all but the beneficent applications of these technologies.

It must be emphasized again that no immediate need to produce more food drives this struggle with nature. In agriculture, at least, more production seems almost a by-product of the insistence on using our science-derived technologies to the hilt—whatever the cost. The current flap over bovine growth hormone is instructive. Awash in milk that was generated by its own policies, the government several years ago funded a dairy herd buyout and killed off or exported 1.62 million dairy cattle (US GAO, 1990c). Now rising milk prices have increased the cost of a government feeding program for poor Women, Infants and Children (WIC), thus increasing the pressure to increase the supply of milk and lower milk prices (Spahr, 1990). *Voila!* Bovine growth hormone to the rescue! Injected into cattle, it will cause each of them to increase milk production significantly, thus moving the system ever closer to the time when a single cow can supply a metropolis (Sun, 1989; Schneider, 1990b).

Author Mark Kramer in *Three Farms,* his brilliant book about the state of American agriculture, provides vivid examples of small farmers and agribusinesses alike trapped in a system where genetically improved cattle, technologically sophisticated cow barns and electronically guided planting and harvesting machines often overproduce milk, pork and tomatoes so that farmers go broke even though the price of food goes up (Kramer, 1977). Modern man's apparent inability to resist newer promises in the face of the substantial social havoc wreaked by technologies already delivered seems to derive from a tendency to identify intentional technological change as an inevitable source of "progress," while intentional social change is widely viewed as antidemocratic, as constraining "freedom." Despite increasing enslavement to technologically supported gigantism, many Americans cling stubbornly to the myth that technology is inherently neutral and hence potentially democratic, while social planning is inherently risky and likely to lead to oppression.

Technology also eliminates guilt. Humans who tried to make things better and failed might have to take the blame. If technology keeps making all the big things worse (while turning out trivial but distracting "improvements" like faster computer printers or faster microwavable meals), it's not really anyone's fault. After all, "you *can't* stop progress." Perhaps a profligate U.S. clings to its myths that science will continue to make things better, and that more technology really will solve the food problem, out of a despairing doubt that goods-addicted Americans will ever be able to bring *themselves* under control.

For that clearly is where the answer lies, although there are few obvious examples of what such self-restrained behavior might look like. Hazel Henderson has suggested that as industrial societies "face up to the unsustainability of their value systems," they need to begin making an inventory of the world's value systems, "since they represent, in essence, packages of social 'software' which produce various mixes of behavioral outputs, technological 'furniture' and organizational forms which can be fitted to specific geographical regions and their ecological carrying capacities" (Henderson, 1981).

One potentially useful value system might be that of the Australian aborigines. Like the Trobriand Islanders whom Malinowski observed (and as with modern industrial societies), they have science. They possess, in the words of one observer, "a systematic body of knowledge regarding their tribal and regional environments. . . . [T]hey know *where* and *when* and *how* to get the food they need." However, in spite of their "accumulated knowledge and skill, and in spite of living according to their appropriate social order, droughts and floods and other untoward circumstances occur; food and water become scarce and life is threatened." The aboriginals know that these things will happen and know that, if possible, they should be prevented. But "without irrigation and conservation . . . without cultivation and animal husbandry, the Aborigines can do no more than express their desire and their need in thought and word, and in action which is social and ritual, but as we see it, without effect. Their interpretation is different. They come to terms with their environment." And they come to terms with it through ritual and symbolism. In seeking to meet their need for food, in other words, the aboriginals traditionally do not seek to control nature, but to control themselves (Elkin, 1964; emphasis added).

It is evident that over most of the globe the human species can no longer survive with such a non-interventionist mind. Each aboriginal could range over scores of miles in seeking food; humans long ago multiplied their numbers to such an extent that without some sort of husbandry (and wifery!) most would starve to death. But neither can humanity survive *without* some such attitude of mind, some way of setting limits on each community's desires and of ccoming to terms with the earth's limited ability to fulfill them.

Uncontrollable Humans

As earlier observed, however, industrial man has viewed his task as the achievement of mastery over, not accommodation with, nature. Leiss (1976) has examined this goal and noted the inherently uneasy relationship between Francis Bacon's recognition that nature might be enslaved to ameliorate the human condition and Thomas Hobbes' assertion that insatiable desire is rooted in the social nature of the human species. If the needs of "civilized" man are indeed insatiable (and U.S. levels of consumption suggest that insatiability can at least be learned), and if certain sectors of humanity have concluded that they must exert increasing control over nature in order to satisfy these insatiable needs, then "we are embarked on an endless enlarging spiral wherein increased control over nature strives to keep pace with burgeoning desire" (Leiss,

1976).

"There is a fundamental paradox here," Leiss goes on, "for this conception describes a species that supposedly cannot exercise any rational control over its own behavior, while simultaneously announcing its intention to subject all of non-human nature to its unchallengeable control through its very rational science and technology. . . . Are we to believe," he asks, "that the gigantic enterprise upon which modern society has embarked resolves itself into a conundrum? That the reason for pursuing human control over all the rest of nature is to enable us finally to unbridle our own nature so that it alone of all things is 'free'?" (Leiss, 1976, p. 39).

Eliot Coleman, perhaps the nation's premier organic food producer, urges his readers to "study the established balances of the natural world" and learn to work within them (Coleman, 1989). The alternative project on which industrial man has embarked seems to be based on an assumption that humanity can set up its *own* balances out of whichever "natural" pieces fit into its constructed world, assuming that nature will continue to keep the whole thing afloat. Most likely nature will not fit in at all. As the Superintendent of Yellowstone Park pointed out after the big fire, "nature regulates more strenuously than human beings might. It seems that we want nature, but don't want it to be entirely natural" (Hackett, 1989). Walt Disney World in Florida recently pleaded guilty to having allowed employees of its Discovery Island (a zoological park with a "natural" environment) to kill, maim, capture and improperly confine" various migratory birds—hawks, falcons, egrets, ibises and the like—that were defecating on its clean park walkways (Bray, 1989).

Brian Stableford, whose visions of production lines turning out rows of headless Chicken Littles or suspended lambchops were described in Chapter 1, makes an argument, the arrogance of which Leiss would surely recognize. "With a really comprehensive knowledge of how biochemical processes are organized and controlled," he writes:

> . . . we should not need to deal with living organisms at all. We may one day be able to produce food substances—and other materials— directly without requiring plants, animals or microorganisms to do it for us. When this happens our relationship with our environment will again be changed profoundly. While we would still be able to control the evolution of any living species, *we would no longer have a pressing need to exploit them in order to supply ourselves with the fundamental necessities of life.* We would be able to respect the natural diversity of species produced by evolution. . . (Stableford,

1984; emphasis added).

In other words, once humans have absolute control, once species have been created to suit every humanly imaginable need, once humans have moved beyond even that to create life in the laboratory, *then* (and presumably only then) can our species afford to respect whichever of nature's creatures have managed to survive manipulation. Only when humanity has achieved total control is it "practical" to imagine leaving nature alone.

The late Malcolm Forbes, one of the world's richest men, once commented on a television show that money was not the source of his happiness. He appears to have achieved the ultimate national fantasy—finally being rich enough to discover that it does not require wealth to be happy. The alternative route to happiness, the view that "it is better to want less than to have more," has proved much less appealing than science's promise that it would eliminate any need for self-control.

Nature as Self-regulator

The conviction that nature *needs* controlling arises out of ignorance. Separated from any direct knowledge of the natural world by unnatural environments, drained of any confidence in common sense by a fruitless search for "scientific answers" to their deepest questions and buffeted as they have been by successive waves of technologically induced change, modern humans have come to view members of not yet domesticated species (from bacteria to mammals) as highly unpredictable, as likely to get out of hand unless kept in check by science. Yet in nature these species control each other and, as noted earlier, life-sustaining activities that are truly essential go forward on the earth without the help of—indeed, despite—the clumsy interference of the human species. Nature's flexibility and reliability is the only thing that has enabled humans to fool around so carelessly for so long without having yet pulled their ecosystem down in ruins around them.

Of course, there is a scale on which nature is, from a human standpoint, unreliable. Insect plagues do appear, rains do fail, devastating plant diseases do wipe out crops. But just as the human capacity for achieving control has been wildly exaggerated, so has the need to achieve such control. Rumors to the contrary notwithstanding, for example, humans have apparently seldom starved simply because nature was fickle. Life-threatening food shortages are rarely, if ever, caused solely by nature, but rather by humans failing to help other humans when local crops failed (Dando, 1980; Brown, 1985). That such mistakes and intentional cruelties occur is in the end the most convincing argument against allowing the "takeover" of nature by humans and corporations run by humans. Over the long term, nature is reliable; humans are not.

Unreliable Humans

The demonstrated incapacity of humans to control and manage large systems safely has been repeatedly demonstrated. (It is hardly impressive that an industry producing power from atoms, barely 40 years old, has had only one globally catastrophic accident!) For all the known reasons (and perhaps many unknown ones as well) the nuclear plant at Chernobyl explodes, the chemical plant at Bhopal leaks, the oil tanker Exxon Valdez hits a reef—radiation, toxic chemicals and crude oil spill. There is an investigation, a trial perhaps, a promise that it will never happen again. But, of course, it will.

A good deal has been written about the vulnerability of large and complex systems. Amory and Hunter Lovins examined the fragility of U.S. energy systems in a truly terrifying book entitled *Brittle Power* (1982). The Lovins' analysis of the vulnerability of this country's existing gas pipeline system to a single terrorist should induce caution about entrusting any part of the food supply to sugar syrup-carrying pipelines. The scary truth about large and complex systems is well expressed in the title of a book by sociologist Charles Perrow, *Normal Accidents* (1984). Large tightly linked systems will "normally" have accidents, he pointed out prophetically, just before Bhopal illustrated the painful truth of his prediction.

In fact, there is no need to merely *speculate* about whether radiation, oil or chemical plant accidents might be models for food system disasters. As Busch reminds us (Busch, 1991), "normal accidents have occurred in the food industry before, the most well-known of which was the unintended insertion of PCBs in animal feed in Michigan." The most well-known, perhaps, but hardly the largest. That distinction may belong to the normal accident that began a decade ago at a packing plant in Billings, Montana, and before it was ended, spread through the food chain into 18 states and British Columbia. (See sidebar.)

Within such initially vulnerable systems, biotechnology presents a special risk. Not only are ways to fully test the safety of its products un-

Source: Joan Gussow, "PCBs for Breakfast and Other Problems with a Food System Gone Awry," *Food Monitor* 2(3), 1985.

This one began in June 1979 when a broken transformer spilled 200 gallons of PCBs into a wastewater system at the Pierce Packing Company in Billings, Montana. By-products scooped from the wastewater were cooked into meat meal for animal food. By the time the problem was discovered, it was necessary to investigate possible contamination in Arizona, California, Idaho, Illinois, Iowa, Kansas, Minnesota, Montana, Nebraska, New Jersey, North Dakota, Ohio, Oregon, Pennsylvania, South Dakota, Utah, Washington, Wisconsin and British Columbia!

A shipment of contaminated industrial grease on its way to Japan was turned back at sea. Seven million eggs, 1.2 million chickens, 30,000 turkeys, 5,300 hogs, two million pounds of industrial grease, 800,000 pounds of animal feed and 74,000 bakery items (as a minimum estimate) had to be destroyed.

What could have happened? How did the pollution spread so far before the problem was detected? As reported in *The New York Times* in September 1979 and in *Science* in January 1980: on July 6, 1979, in a routine inspection, a government poultry inspector sampled the chickens at Jolly Wholesale Poultry in Provo, Utah. He put the samples in a freezer and went on vacation for seven days. Five days after he returned the samples arrived at a San Francisco testing laboratory, where, after 10 days of testing, it was discovered that there was a problem: the chicken samples contained *five times the allowed levels* of PCB.

Nine days later these samples arrived at the Meat and Poultry inspection regional office in Alameda. Three days later the agency's office in Boulder, Colorado, got word of the contamination. It took nine days to trace the chickens back to Jolly Wholesale Poultry. Five days later PCB was found in meat meal and a week later—59 days after samples were taken—the company announced it would destroy the contaminated chickens. It took twelve more days to trace the contamination to the leaking transformer at Pierce Packing Company in Billings, Montana, by which time the PCBs had been consumed by a variety of humans and animals.

A study by the Office of Technology Assessment concluded that despite an apparently elaborate system of safeguards, there have been a frightening number of such incidents involving "wide distribution and partial consumption of food" tainted with chemicals never intended to enter the food chain. We are assured that so far there is no imminent threat to public health, although it is unclear just what that means when the import of the OTA report is that no one is really sure who has eaten how much of what. It has been suggested that the FDA should set up pilot programs to look for "unanticipated" chemicals in the food supply, though the cost is daunting: two million dollars for each state or regional laboratory set up to look for "unanticipated chemicals" and the cost for testing for each "unanticipated" chemical is about $10,000.

defined, but one of the "strongest sources of early hazard identification [,] informed but independent basic scientists," may be hard to come by. A disturbing characteristic of the technologies that have "dominated the innovation process," Robert Kates pointed out to the NAS several years ago, is "the blurring of roles between basic scientist, technologist and entrepreneur. . . .[S]cientists knowledgeable about a technology, but not intertwined with its development or production are societies' early hazard warning system. Missing them, we are due for some surprises in these attractive technological fields" (Kates, 1985).

Once again it is not necessary to speculate about *possible* "surprises." The "attractive" and very new field of biotechnology has already seen an intentional non-release of possibly damaging information on the part of interested scientists. In 1989, a mysterious outbreak of illness that ultimately killed 27 people and afflicted 1,535 others was rather rapidly traced to the use of an amino acid, L-tryptophan as a dietary supplement. It was traced somewhat more slowly to specific batches of that supplement made by a Japanese company over a particular time period. What was not publicly revealed until almost nine months later was that the deadly tryptophan was produced by gene splicing.

According to the journal *Science,* Food and Drug Administration "officials were apparently hoping to keep the recombinant link quiet until they could determine whether it in fact did play a role in the outbreak" (Roberts, 1990). But as an indignant letter to *Science* subsequently pointed out, the "idea of FDA scientists suppressing vital health information out of a concern for the impact on the biotechnology industry does little to inspire confidence in the FDA as a regulator of this new technology" (Mellon, 1990).

In a too seldom cited book, *Filters Against Folly,* biologist Garrett Hardin writes that one of the skills citizens need if they wish to recapture from "experts" the ability to make judgments about their world is "ecolacy." This neologism he draws from parallels with "literacy" (the ability to understand words) and "numeracy" (an understanding of numbers). To be *ecolate,* he argues, is to understand connections and consequences, to be able to ask of any proposed solution, "And *then* what?" Reading about a cascading disaster like the one that began in Billings or a toxic surprise like the bacteria-generated L-tryptophan, reminds us forcibly that "and then what?" is a question that ought to lead, as Hardin suggests, to "caution and humility. . . the hallmarks of the ecolate attitude toward the world" (Hardin, 1985).

Compare his attitude with that of Stableford (1984) commenting on the need to develop bacteria that can convert cellulose to "valuable materials." We must, of course, be very careful with such materials, he warns, since "if the bacteria inside those fermenters ever got out, there could be an ecocatastrophe of spectacular dimensions." Yet the possibility of inadvertently converting all vegetation to something else does not appear to suggest to Stableford the human species' need for more time to ask "and then what?" One is reminded of novelist Kurt Vonnegut's "innocent" scientist in *Cat's Cradle,* who, trying to solve the army's swamp problem by inventing a crystal that could turn water into an unmeltable solid, ended life on earth when the crystal accidentally escaped (Vonnegut, 1963).

The possibility of human failure in such dangerous systems—that the personnel watching the fermenters will fail to notice something vital—is, of course, the reason why the replacement of humans by something that seems more manageable (a machine or a robot) is always viewed as progress by the same man-made corporations that are most eager to manage nature. In that sense, ordinary humans are—from the corporation's standpoint—part of nature and equally in need of control. And when managers begin to recognize the limits to their own abilities, they are forced to relinquish the management of the largest and most complex systems to computers—which are not, as we have all learned, *fool*-proof—or even proof against the wise. It is no accident that the futurist fantasies of the technophiles are about civilizations in which computers that have become smarter than themselves, take over (to their relief), guiding humanity through the shoals of the technoworld it has created.

Much of the technosphere is currently embedded in systems so complicated that they must of necessity be managed with computers. These tell their keepers through monitors what they are doing. And as watching monitors becomes routine, these watchers are more easily distracted. And, perhaps most fatally, as more of us for more of the time become simply passive watchers, the less we have actually to do, and the less likely we are to act. In such circumstances, a "deviation" from the norm is likely to become just "something wrong with the computer." The "worst ever" oil leak into New York harbor off Staten Island came from a pipeline, the leak detection alarm of which "had been malfunctioning for at least a year." When the spill occurred, the presumably faulty detector gave two warning signals, but—inured by false alarms—nobody reacted, and half a million gallons of oil went into the Arthur Kill (Wolff, 1990).

Nature is reliable because it is *complex;* that complexity allows it to respond to surprises (which in human systems are "accidents") by finding another way of doing what must get done. Human systems are merely *complicated*. They have no intentions, except to return to a "natural" state. When they break free of human control to do that, the consequences are most likely to be quite different from those their human designers intended, for example, Bhopal, where humans were maimed and killed by a gas meant for killing "pests."

Nature is not only more reliable, but a good deal more self-reliant and clever than has previously been understood. Only recently has agricultural science even thought to begin inventorying her skills. Weeds now turn out to have complex and often helpful effects on crop plants—reducing insect populations, increasing numbers of helpful predators, concentrating certain nutrients (Weeds In Pest . . . , 1982). Many plants have the ability to alter the environment around their own roots—sometimes with the help of various soil fungi or root-colonizing bacteria—so as to make better use of available nutrients or more effectively resist attack by insects and diseases (Schroth and Hancock, 1982; Harley and Russell, 1979). Trees have the capacity to produce leaves of different nutritional and taste characteristics on different branches, thus reducing the efficiency of their insect predators who, moving about among the leaves, expose themselves to *their* enemies (Stipanovic, 1982).

That nature has such abilities is humanity's good fortune, since the inescapable truth is that nature is, and will continue to be, in charge; humans can do little more than try to understand and work with her. Technologically induced change cannot, therefore, be permitted to casually destroy pieces of the system not immediately useful to humans, as if we had a celestial contract assuring us that anything "natural" that is currently useful to our species would go on functioning normally. The war being waged by technology against nature can probably be won if humanity simply continues on its present path, but the post-war world will be grim.

As the next chapter shows, in some areas around the country there is support for, and belief in, food systems that work with nature and are ecologically and socially sustainable. End-of-the-decade events in Eastern Europe have, moreover, strengthened the hope that dramatic and unpredictable changes of attitude can occur. Yet, as the Rogoff and Rawlins' scenario demonstrates, powerful forces continue to drive the nation toward production systems from which all natural variability has been effectively excluded. "Cloning Offers Factory Precision to the Farm" is a headline of hope to such forces—not a warning (Schneider,

1988). Considering more conservative alternatives to their own vision of a radically changed food system, Rogoff and Rawlins came up with the "extension of existing technology to 100-acre controlled environment domes" (see Chapter 4, page 49). Little room here for cooperation with nature!

And when the food emerges from the domes or the fermentation tanks, there will be companies waiting who believe that what the public wants is "a whole new class of processed foods that are not just quick and tasty, but designed to prevent disease . . ."; foods custom designed "to match your specific health requirements" that could be delivered to your door, like pizza (Rohlfing, 1990). What will prevent a public, already alienated from nature, from arriving at the conclusion that "foods" like these—foods not dependent on agriculture as we understand it—are not only feasible but desirable, that the best foods are those produced with the fewest concessions to the living world?

7.

GETTING FROM HERE TO
WHERE WE NEED TO BE

Eliot Coleman's recent book *The New Organic Grower* provided me with the following quotation, which says with great succinctness what was laid out at much greater length in the previous chapter:

> The miraculous succession of modern inventions has so profoundly affected our thinking as well as our everyday life that it is difficult for us to conceive that the ingenuity of men will not be able to solve the final riddle—that of gaining a subsistence from the earth. The grand and ultimate illusion would be that man would provide a substitute for the elemental working of nature.
>
> — Fairfield Osborn, *Our Plundered Planet*

Osborne wrote that in 1948. Nothing written almost half a century later about the problems we face in coming to terms with nature is really new, except that we are further down the wrong road, we are more profoundly de-natured and the accelerating rate at which technology reshapes our lives keeps undercutting our ability even to imagine a different sort of world. One other thing has changed, however. Some fraction of humanity, including a meaningful fraction of the scientific establishment, is becoming humblingly aware that our civilization is adversely affecting the biosphere, and that none of us is certain what can be done about it (Benedick, 1990).

Readers will recall my pointing out in Chapter 1 that Del Monte's promotion of Hawaiian Punch and Farm Aid in the same advertisement was predicated on an assumption of absolute public ignorance of how food and agriculture now fit together. So you will anticipate the statement I am about to make. Just as buying Hawaiian punch will not help save the family farm, neither will it be saved by simply teaching consumers to purchase foods labeled "pesticide-free," "natural" or even "organically grown." The preceding chapters were meant to assert that simply getting people worried about the purity of what they put into their stomachs will not be enough to save the food system unless they can also be taught two other things. First, they need to learn much more than they presently know about where, how, when and by whom their food is produced. Second, they need to know what they can do to influence that.

In this book I have raised the question: Is there a Chicken Little in our future? And I have concluded that there well might be unless people can be brought to fight against it. How can that be done? I pointed out in Chapter 1 that a series of events raising questions about the safety of their food supply has led some consumers to demand foods, especially fruits and vegetables, that are free of chemical residues. Chapter 2 documented that the agricultural system of which consumers are making this demand is being driven by both economic and environmental concerns to make significantly lower use of chemical inputs. In Chapter 3, I observed that it is possible to address the farming problems—as with other resource constraints we face—in at least two major ways. One of these, which has been called a soft path or a Sane-Humane-Ecological approach, endeavors to find ways of provisioning the race by working *with* nature. The other approach, which can be seen as an extension and elaboration of present trends, involves creating ever more sophisticated technologies to regulate those parts of the food system that remain under nature's control.

Chapter 4 offers one biotech vision of what a food system made "sustainable" by human ingenuity might look like. In Chapter 5, I argue that while I do not actually believe that a Chicken Little production line or a system for growing tomato sauce in vats in Rahway, New Jersey, will ever entirely replace the farming system we presently have, there is no obvious reason why it should not. Reading about the progress of biotechnology and the money and passion invested in its wonders, it becomes impossible to assert with any conviction that such unlikely end points could not be attained since much of the present food supply would have seemed as improbable to our great grandparents as Chicken Little may now seem to us. Moreover, since production agriculture is to many city dwellers almost as exotic as Chicken Little production lines, fear alone is as likely to lead the public in the direction of fabricated foods that are both pure *and* disease preventing, as it is to lead them toward the more "natural" products of a sustainable farming system.

Finally, in Chapter 6, I tried to show why Chicken Little would not only fail to solve world hunger, but why any "solution" that required—or allowed—a takeover of nature by corporations would probably threaten human survival. "Designer" foods are end products of an ongoing search for absolute control over the food system, a search that is both futile—and dangerous. And the corporations engaged in that quest, the folks who now actually control much of our food supply, are the very operations who run ads capitalizing on our sentimental view of farmers.

Who Controls the Food System?

So the bad news is that anyone hoping for a smaller-scale, relocalized food system must come to terms with the fact that the same industries that have long controlled the production (and encouraged the over-use) of energy, fertilizers and pesticides now also control germplasm (seeds) and much of the biotechnology research as well (Doyle, 1985). And down on what used to be the farm, it is discomforting to realize that where hundreds of thousands of small farmers once raised chickens out back, there is now *the $16 billion-a-year chicken industry* that controls every aspect of chicken production from feedmills and hatcheries, to 20,000 contract farmers who "grow out" the chicks, to processing plants where 150,000 (largely black, largely women) workers gut, cut up and package more than 100 million fryers a week (Hall, 1989). In 1960, 286 companies sold commercially raised fryers to retail marketers; such firms now number fewer than 50 (Black, 1990). Think of the labor discontent that could be eliminated if one of these giants were to perfect Chicken Little.

The largest food company in the U.S., the largest advertiser *and* the largest producer of consumer goods in the world (Krebs, 1989) is now Philip Morris, producer of Marlboro, "sponsor" of the Bill of Rights, which has bought up General Foods and Kraft among others. (The third largest food company is RJR Nabisco—RJR for RJ Reynolds, a tobacco company.) It is probably relevant to note that Philip Morris has instructed a major food subsidiary not to include smoking cessation in health programs for its employees and for years blocked the showing of a film titled "Death in the West" in which former Marlboro cowboys can be seen dying of emphysema and cancer. At a minimum these actions demonstrate the reach of corporate power, and an indifference to our health by the companies that now control the food system.

Those warm and friendly "homestyle" products in the supermarket have succumbed to acquisition frenzy. The kitchens of Mrs. Paul and Pepperidge Farms already belong to Campbell. Laura Scudder hangs out at Borden and Mrs. Smith at Kellogg. It sometimes seems as if only Paul Newman still belongs to himself. A financial analyst, speculating about "how the Philip Morris buyup of Kraft might affect our future eating habits, observed that one 'could well start with a Miller Lite beer, eat a whole meal, then light up a Marlboro after you get done,' and never have to use a product outside the new behemoth" (Krebs, 1989).

The sheer size of these companies is disturbing; industries operating on that scale need control and uniformity to function at all. Control and uniformity—factory values—work against the astonishing subtlety and variety characteristic of (and essential to) natural systems. They tend to erase the regional and cultural (and *agri*cultural) differences that enrich our lives and the taste of our food. Such giant industries also tend to be anti-democratic and, like dinosaurs, seem to be too big to notice what they are doing to the natural and social environments they lumber through.

Thus the systems now in place to produce and process our food appear to be leading us toward a future that is not only unnatural and dangerous, but one in which our food will be controlled by corporate entities that have often acted to date as if they are unconcerned about the health and safety of humans or the survival of the global ecosystem. What can be done? What is, in fact, being done?

The standard answer to that question, as I said, is to assume that the system can be changed by teaching ever more citizens to demand healthful food. That assumption seems questionable. For the real issue here is not food safety, personal health or even food abundance. The real issue is the survival of the planet, an outcome that requires paying attention to fundamental economic, social, cultural and biological relationships that are quite invisible to the food shopper. The food system will not automatically evolve into something more democratic and benign, even if most of us begin to buy organic food at farmers' markets. If consumers demand pesticide-free food, large corporations are capable of devoting some small fraction of their land to the "organic market" and saturating that market until depressed prices drive the smaller producers out (Whynott, 1989). And when recession turns con-

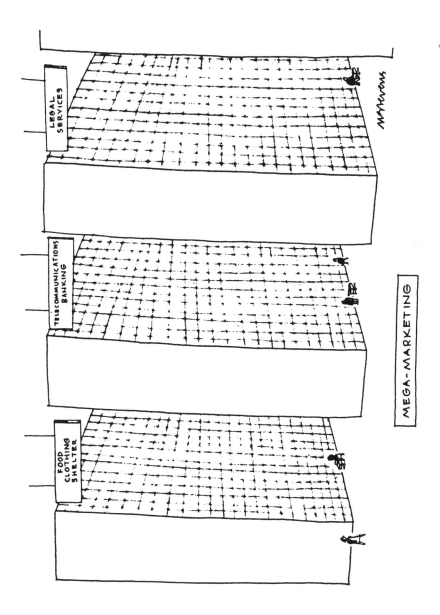

Drawing by M. Stevens; © 1988
The New Yorker Magazine, Inc.

sumers away from food that costs more in the market today—even if it is a long-term environmental bargain—big producers have the resources to hold on. The forces moving the system toward gigantism will not give up without a fight.

The food supply, I have come to believe, will not be saved by trying to save the supply itself, but by engaging eaters in the race to save the planet.* Food is simply a lens through which the connections between other problems can be understood. People concerned only about the food they put into their own stomachs are likely to be fairweather friends of agriculture, but people concerned about the environment will almost inevitably become engaged in helping sustain the systems that supply their food.

Before confronting the issue of how environmentally alarmed citizens might be engaged in the battle against the denaturing corporations that are now in control of food, it seems important to review briefly the very real achievements of the last decade, during which a constituency for reform in the food system has developed among representatives of two groups of people: producers themselves and a much larger group—ordinary consumers of food. There are hopeful trends among both of these groups, but since it all begins with farmers, we too will begin with food production.

The Mainstreaming of Sustainable Agriculture

As was implied in the the report to the Governors in Chapter 2, there is a growing understanding among producers that agriculture *must* change, must (at a minimum) move rapidly toward more environmentally benign methods of producing food. During Jimmy Carter's presidency, following decades during which the U.S. Department of Agriculture considered "organic" production methods beneath notice, an agricultural policy analyst named Garth Youngberg was hired to take a serious look at "organic" production as it was practiced around the world. As a member of a task force appointed by Secretary of Agriculture Robert Berglund, Youngberg helped examine the viability of a

---

* This has not in the past dissuaded a colleague and myself from urging nutrition educators to try to help save the food supply. (See Appendix: Dietary Guidelines for Sustainability.)

range of farming systems generally grouped under the adjective "organic." The task force produced a landmark document, *Report and Recommendations on Organic Farming* (USDA, 1980), which—despite the disapproval of an incoming administration that did not favor such "outdated" approaches to farming—generated 40,000 requests for copies and was translated into seven foreign languages (Youngberg, 1989). In 1989, asked to speak to an audience attending a special symposium on ecology and agriculture in Salina, Kansas, Youngberg looked back from the rim of a new decade and marveled at "The Mainstreaming of Sustainable Agriculture" that had taken place in the intervening years.

"Try to think back to the fall of 1979," he urged his listeners, and then reminded them what the agricultural world looked like:

- There was virtually no research on sustainable agriculture going on. . . .

- There was virtually no dialogue between the proponents of an alternative agriculture and the so-called agricultural establishment.

- There were virtually no institutions addressing the issues of a more sustainable agriculture.

- There was virtually no recognition of the need to even begin talking about the importance of these issues.

Yet since then, Youngberg noted, the organic farming report had come out, a score of land grant universities had developed "recognizable programs in sustainable agriculture" and the number of states with legislation certifying organically grown foods had grown to 20. Moreover, a farm bill containing important conservation provisions, and $4.5 million for low-input sustainable-agriculture (LISA) research and development, had passed Congress in 1985. And now, Youngberg told his 1989 audience, the prestigous National Academy of Sciences Board on Agriculture had issued a landmark report that was interpreted as a ringing endorsement of a spectrum of low-input agricultural practices (NRC, 1989). Perhaps even more startling, a spokesman for an administration that had once declared itself hostile to such initiatives—and fired Youngberg—publicly endorsed "alternative agriculture." "Sustainable agriculture," Youngberg noted, was the most "prominent buzz word in Washington as the debate over the 1990 farm bill approached . . ." He goes on:

> . . . [T]here are very positive signs of change. In the past ten years
> we've gone from an environment of great uncertainty, of tremendous
> conflict, virtually no dialogue, a period of darkness to at least 1,000
> points of light; and these lights are getting brighter every day.
>
> Minds are changing very rapidly. Individual scientists at the bench
> level are reevaluating their missions. Farmers are reevaluating their
> cropping systems and their futures. Policymakers are begining to
> create a more level policy playing field, and consumers are demand-
> ing a cleaner and safer food supply (Youngberg, 1989).

Six months after Youngberg assured his audience that the approaches to crop production generically referred to as "sustainable" are
now mainstream, an Assistant Secretary of Agriculture went so far as
to acknowledge that sustainable agriculture management practices met
even the free-marketer's criterion of acceptability; they were compatible with American competitiveness in world trade (*Nutrition Week,*
1990). Subsequently, a 1990 Farm Bill that contained a number of "conservation" provisions increased the LISA program authorization from
$4.5 to $40 million (LISA Funding, 1990).

The "recognizable" programs in sustainable agriculture at land
grant universities, the NRC report on *Alternative Agriculture,* organic
certification programs that exist or are being seriously considered in
more than half the states, the increased USDA funding and the inclusion
of an organic definition in the 1990 farm bill—all these are signs that
economics (and ecological concerns) are driving farmers toward a future "with fewer chemicals and more concern for protecting natural
resources" (*Prodigal Crops,* 1988).

But the future is not yet here. Youngberg himself has been quoted
as estimating that the number of farms that have either stopped using
chemicals or are in transition to doing so is 20,000 to 50,000, which
means that no more than 2 percent of the 2.2 million farms have begun
to make the transition to chemical-free agriculture (US GAO, 1990a).
And his estimate is higher than the 1 percent usually cited as the fraction of agriculture that is now "organic" (Whynott, 1989). Although
farm programs that encourage specific crops have been blamed for the
system's resistance to change, farmers' decisions about whether to
adopt "alternative" methods are also strongly affected by their belief
that such methods require more management, more work and unavail-
able labor, while producing more weeds along with declining yields and
profits (US GAO, 1990a).

Moreover, farmers' reasons for turning away from chemicals are not merely environmental, or even economic. They are, in many cases, purely practical. Many entomologists recognized early on that pesticides could not continue to work in the long run, since pests reproduce in such numbers that genetically resistant strains tend to evolve very rapidly (Perkins, 1982). Because the emphasis on other methods of pest management is so long overdue, it may not be unduly optimistic to conclude, as did the Governor's report in Chapter 2: "We'll have a fairly chemical free agriculture in 20 years" (*Prodigal Crops*, 1988, p. 18). Even that will not be achieved without a battle, however, since the chemical companies and their supporters are fighting back against the consumer perception that agricultural chemicals pose any risk to consumers or the environment.*

A genuinely *sustainable* agriculture must be much more than simply chemical-free. Yet a food system that uses less chemicals and is therefore less polluting of land, water and food can probably be achieved without necessarily satisfying other criteria for sustainability—which, at the very least, ought to include conservation of such limited resources as topsoil, water and energy.

The Governors' report in Chapter 2 notes further that "sustainable agriculture came out of the drive to preserve moderate- and family-size farms as economically viable and socially desirable." Thus the social agenda outlined on page 26 of Chapter 2 was among the driving forces behind the move toward a new approach to farming. This fact was made explicit in a widely circulated statement on sustainable agriculture adopted by participants at the Ecological Farming Conference in Asilomar, California, in January of 1990. The first of "Seven Challenges" for sustainable agriculture was to "[p]romote and sustain healthy rural communities" (Asilomar Declaration. . . , 1990). Such a social agenda is obviously in conflict with those whose goals are merely "chemical-free" agriculture.

In short, there is an ongoing dialogue over just exactly what "sus-

---

* For example, a special issue of *Fruit Grower* produced by the editors of *American Fruit Grower*, including *Eastern Fruit Grower*, dated Summer 1990 carries a cover illustration showing against a background of fruits a large "Tested & Approved Safe" logo with the subtitle "Stamp Out the Uncertainty." The editorial inside the front cover, headed "Growers Must Get Involved," indicates that the sponsors of "this special effort" are ICI America, Du Pont and Rhone-Poulenc, all manufacturers of agricultural chemicals. Their message is *not* that chemical use must be reduced.

tainable" means in addition to "lowering chemical inputs." (See, for example, Lockeretz, 1988; Crosson, 1989; Madden, 1989; Enshayan, 1990.) Lockeretz points out that there is no empirical evidence supporting the notion that small to moderate is the appropriate size for "sustainable" farms; and the recognition that larger scale "organic" farming may increasingly rely on outside sources of energy/fertility is a reminder that even "organic" agriculture need not necessarily be "sustainable" (Whynott, 1989). And as the discussion continues, much of the agricultural system is still losing topsoil at unacceptable rates, still overusing and polluting ground and surface waters and still losing farms and farmers as it staggers toward gigantism (*Farm Bill,* 1990).

Yet efforts designed to help create the social and political bases for a sustainable system are also gaining adherents. In Walthill, Nebraska, the Center for Rural Affairs takes seriously the mandate to think globally and act locally, turning out analyses of unsustainable agricultural policies and practices in Nebraska,and organizing local farmers to battle corporate agriculture. And across the midwest, groups like the Land Stewardship Project work to increase public awareness of the need for an ethical stance toward the use of the land.

And while the relocalization of the food supply was a truly unimaginable idea 20 years ago at a time when the dominant image— that of the global supermarket—seemed unassailable, interest in sustaining local agriculture was stimulated by the oil crisis of the 1970s. In the mid-1970s, the New England states and others that lacked the climatic advantages (and the subsidized water) of California began to realize that a very high percentage of their perishable food was imported from long distances—usually by petroleum-burning trucks, using a questionably reliable bridge and highway system (Baumel and Hayenga, 1984). In such states as Massachusetts in the northeast and Texas in the southwest, state agriculture commissioners like Augustus (Gus) Schumacher and Jim Hightower* began to move toward changing the policies that had helped destroy local agriculture in their own states.

As a consequence of efforts by the Massachusetts Department of Agriculture, for example, Massachusetts by 1986, for the first time in history, ranked first in New England in dollars earned from agriculture.

---

* Between the time this was written and presstime, Jim Hightower was voted out of office and Gus Schumacher resigned. The decision to retain mention of their initiatives in the chapter reflects the view that they remain signposts to a viable future.

Since this accomplishment was built partly on the backs of other states that were doing less well, the more optimistic statistic might be that in 1988 the number of farms in Massachusetts may actually have increased, rather than declined. In his introduction to *The Massachusetts Farm and Food System: A Five-Year-Policy Framework 1989-1993*, Commissioner Schumacher noted that despite this improvement, the state still imported 85 percent of its food. The state agriculture department, planned, therefore, to continue implementing measures that could help preserve the farmland base and to increase farm profitability, with the intention of increasing the number of farms in the state from 6,000 to 6,500 by 1993.

In Texas, former Agriculture Commissioner Hightower's efforts to sustain local agriculture included a heavy emphasis on promoting diversity. He urged farmers not to "go on raising cows and wheat and hay if there's no market for it," (Schutze, 1989) but to move into alternative crops like deer, ostriches, emus, alligators, table grapes and watermelons as well as such ethnic market crops as those grown at Cambodian Gardens, Inc., the 100th Texas Certified Organic farm—lemon grass, bitter melon, water spinach, long beans and Thai peppers (Antosh, 1989; Gazette, 1990). "People tend to think of these as kind of cute projects," Hightower said about efforts of this sort, "but in fact, they're big income producers" (McAfee and Waldman, 1988).

Moves to rebuild the local farm base usually start from a recognition that this renewed agriculture must be organic or sustainable. In Texas, where Hightower declared 1989 "The Year of Sustainable Agriculture" (Mann and Yarrow, 1990), what has been described as the toughest organic certification bill in the nation pushes farmers toward severing their dependence on chemicals (Schutze, 1989). In Massachusetts 1993 goals include expanded compost production and a 50 percent reduction in toxic chemical use through the use of integrated pest management (IPM) and the development of environmentally safe biological pesticides and disease-resistant (as opposed to pesticide-tolerant) crops.

Agricultural renewal efforts in rapidly urbanizing states tend to be pushed toward "organic" by the fact that organically labeled produce almost always brings a premium on the market. This allows small farmers—cultivating land that would be more valuable under houses than under vegetables—to make a living on vegetables. Whether these state efforts will be "sustainable" in the economic sense if development pressures continue to encourage farmers to sell out and retire will depend on just how important states and their citizens deem it to main-

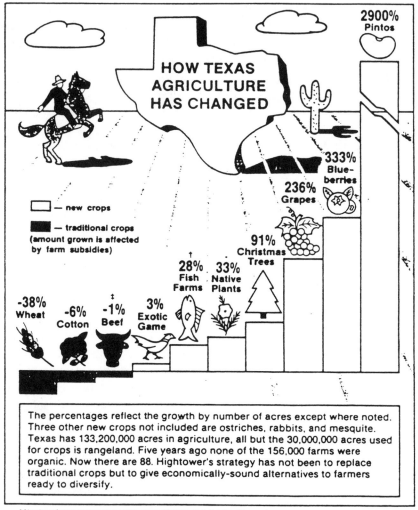

The percentages reflect the growth by number of acres except where noted. Three other new crops not included are ostriches, rabbits, and mesquite. Texas has 133,200,000 acres in agriculture, all but the 30,000,000 acres used for crops is rangeland. Five years ago none of the 156,000 farms were organic. Now there are 88. Hightower's strategy has not been to replace traditional crops but to give economically-sound alternatives to farmers ready to diversify.

* Number of wholesale growers; † Number of fish farms; ‡ Number of animals.

Chart by Leslie Flis from *Organic Gardening*, December 1989. Reprinted with permission.

tain a local food-producing capacity.

Efforts to maintain such a capacity may in some cases be supported by state and local agencies in addition to agriculture departments, since states have a number of reasons the federal government does not have for keeping local farmers in business. A major one is the fact that farms help maintain open space in crowded areas of the country. A number of states, particularly in the northeast, have developed state food or food and agriculture plans, sometimes, as in New York, under the leadership of the State Department of Health with the cooperation of other departments and agencies (New York State, n.d.). Those interested in helping to create a sustainable food system need to examine their state food and nutrition plans to ensure that they support local food production. This can be accomplished by encouraging the use of local foods and food products in situations where the state has a say in purchasing or influencing the purchase of food, for example, in such programs as school lunch, elderly feeding programs, prisons and the like.

In Massachusetts, use of local produce in a variety of private as well as public settings is encouraged by *The Green Book: A Directory of Wholesale Growers of Massachusets Grown and Fresher Products,* issued in 1990 as a guide to wholesale buyers for local restaurants, foodstores and institutional food service. It is heartening to see a list of growers of tomatoes, radishes and swiss chard, mustard greens and raspberries in a highly industrial, densely populated northeastern state (*Green Book,* 1990).

Interest in and support for the maintenance of local agriculture has also been generated by extra-governmental groups and individuals. In the early 1980s, the late Robert Rodale's Cornucopia Project developed a simple model—using national food consumption data—for analyzing food self-reliance at the state level and showing how local production could substitute for foods now imported into the state (Pennsylvania Food . . . , n.d.; Cornucopia Project, 1981; Pahl, 1982). More recently, a retired business executive decided to promote Connecticut agriculture by engaging a local nutritionist to develop a series of seasonal menus that met the current nutritional guidelines for cancer prevention. The researchers then calculated the size of the potential market that could be created if all the foods included were produced locally (Stephens, et al., 1988).

In Montana, one researcher investigated the state's history of food production in order to determine the extent to which the state had ever been self-reliant in food. The lists she generated of foods previously grown in Montana were used by local agricultural agents to encourage bank loans to farmers who wished to begin production of such crops again (Herrin and Gussow, 1989). In Maine, a law originated by the local organic farmers association encourages purchase of locally grown organic produce by requiring retailers to label produce possibly treated with post-harvest chemicals or imported from countries that used banned U.S. pesticides (*Safe Food . . . ,* 1989).

Although the state is the governmental unit of convenience—legislatures and governors govern states, and statistics are kept at the state rather than the regional level—there is also a movement to relocalize agriculture based on the notion of bioregions (Sale, 1985). Despite the fact that the definition and boundaries of bioregions are not yet cleanly defined, a serious bioregional movement exists, coordinated by the North American Bioregional Congress.

There are, in short, a variety of efforts in both the private and the public sectors to help create a more sustainable food-producing system. But the constituency for reform of the food system that has developed over the last decade or so has also involved consumers, whose role, of course, is critical.

Consumers as Reformers in the Food System

The greatest contribution consumers have made to the maintenance of local agriculture has been their direct purchasing from farmers at country farmstands or at urban farmers' markets where, depending on the market rules, only local farmers can participate, selling only what they produce. According to a *New York Times* article on farmers' markets, *American Demographics* magazine estimated that in 1990 consumers would purchase food directly from 200,000 farmers at farmstands and farmers' markets (Farmers' Markets . . . , 1990). The Public Markets Collaborative, a privately funded group that works to establish and sustain urban markets, reported recently that the number of such markets has doubled in the decade of the 1980s (Baum, 1991).

City markets are often encouraged by state or municipal governments, and even the federal government has helped by funding a Federal Farmers' Market Coupon program in ten states that supplies vouchers to low-income citizens for use at farmers' markets. In Massachusetts, two farmstands issued their own vouchers. "Invest now in your summer cravings for Berkshire grown plants and veggies" says the promotional literature for Berkshire Farm Preserve Notes. At a cost of $9, these notes are redeemable for $10 worth of fruits, vegetables and plants the following year. The farmers will invest the money in such winter costs as heating greenhouses.

What is known as Community Supported Agriculture (CSA) requires an even greater level of investment in the future. In the CSA approach, which aims "not just to raise food but also to raise consciousness" (Groh and McFaden, 1990), families join together to

A Berkshire Farm Preserve Note — a $10 note redeemable for plants and produce. "REDEEMABLE FOR PLANTS AND PRODUCE UP TO A VALUE OF TEN DOLLARS — A BERKSHIRE FARM PRESERVE NOTE — IN FARMS WE TRUST"

This note is redeemable for plants and produce up to a value of ten dollars at

Taft Farms
Rte. 183
Great Barrington, Massachusetts

Corn Crib
Rte. 7
Sheffield, Massachusetts

Redeemable Only From *May 1990* to *Oct 1990*

Donald M. Zigler

in cooperation with SHARE, 195 Main Street, Great Barrington, MA 01230

economically support a farmer while the farmer produces food for the families. Although the practice was first introduced into New England in 1986, interest has been sufficiently high that there are now close to 200 farms functioning under such an arrangement (Shouldice, 1991). Basically, a farmer figures out what it will cost him or her to grow produce for a specific number of families (sometimes dairy cattle, chickens and other livestock are included), including a reasonable salary for the farmer. The cost is divided up among the families who pay, usually up front, to receive produce throughout the spring, summer and fall. Provisions are made by each CSA group for handling surpluses, differences of taste and so on. Shareholders stop by "their" farm once or twice a week to pick up produce, or they may have it

delivered to some mutually convenient central location. During the growing season they may help plant, pick or weed; in the winter, they plan for the following season.

It is clear that customers at farmers' markets and farmstands appreciate both fresh produce and contact with farmers, as do participants in CSA projects. But while public markets may save many a downtown, and while farmstands and CSA projects may significantly improve and/or guarantee the incomes of small farmers, one cannot be overly sanguine about the impact of such direct purchase arrangements on the food system as a whole. The first reason is that despite their growing popularity, farmer's markets are a drop in the food system bucket. While the number of downtown markets may have doubled in 1990, the doubling was from 1,200 to 2,000 in a country with over 40,000 communities large enough to have post offices.

Most fruits and vegetables are still sold in supermarkets. And although many of these have posted signs assuring consumers that products come from local and/or organic farms, and have responded to consumer food safety concerns by participating in certification programs guaranteeing their produce to be "residue-free," such assurances are usually found only in the produce sections of supermarkets.

Which brings us to the second reason why farmers' markets—even if they accounted for a significant fraction of produce sales—can have so little impact on the food system. Most supermarket shelves are not filled with produce, but with a range of other products with an often tenuous relationship to farming. The brutal fact is that farmers cannot save the food system by selling directly to consumers because consumers use so little in unprocessed form of what farmers produce. Crop production is largely driven by exporter, livestock feeder or processor demands—not by the demands of ordinary eaters. Therefore, in order to save us from the likes of Chicken Little, consumers will have to care about production agriculture, as an ecological, political and social factor in their lives, not merely as the immediate source of some of the food objects they put into their own mouths. For those things are, as Rogoff and Rawlins point out, mere "condiments" in the system as a whole.

Concern—and wisdom—about the workings of the whole food system are probably greatest among an unmeasured segment of the consuming public already deeply involved in various issues that occupy the food and agriculture interface: food and nutrition policy, economic justice, farmworker dignity and safety, humane treatment of animals as well as the issue with the largest and most powerful, constituency—the environment. Many of the groups that have been organized to express such food-related concerns are listed in a volume, now in its third edition, *Healthy Harvest III: A Directory of Sustainable Agriculture & Horticulture Organizations, 1989-1990*. It carries a list of 1,000 organizations (up from 300 in its first edition) involved with everything from rural development in the Philippines (Abra Diocesan Rural Development), to the distribution from Los Altos, California, of organically grown produce to the U.S. and Canada (Your Land, Our Land, Inc.). Interested readers are likely to find in *Healthy Harvest* one or more organizations in which they may wish to participate. (Both the Center for Rural Affairs and the Land Stewardship Project, for example, are listed, as is Community Supported Agriculture.)

Cooperation or . . . Disaster?

It is important to ask whether coalitions of the members, supporters or mere spiritual adherents of groups such as those described above are going to save us from a "Chicken Little" future. Unquestionably, individuals concerned with helping develop a more sustainable food system will be more effective if they participate in or contribute to a group working toward some related end than if they simply complain as individuals to local supermarket managers about the lack of organic produce or the excessive space given over to heavily sweetened breakfast cereals. The supermarket manager will stock what sells, no matter how many complaints are received.

But if consumers are actually to change the system, they will need to refuse to buy much of what is offered, and they must refuse in large enough numbers that their refusal forces change both in the fields *and* in the factories. That this kind of power can be achieved by consumers has been demonstrated by a Japanese cooperative, the Seikatsu Club, which won last year's honorary Alternative Nobel Prize (Right Livelihood . . . , 1989). The goals of the Seikatsu Club—environmentally conscious purchasing decisions, reduction in irrational product variety, sustainably produced safe food, community building and the empowerment of women—seem more ambitiously encompassing than most existing U.S. co-ops could conceivably embrace.

The club began in 1965 when a Tokyo housewife, upset by the high cost of milk, organized 200 women to buy milk collectively. From that 200-member informal milk-buying collective has grown a 200,000-member food-buying collective, which has moved from the simple goal of saving money to the much more ambitious goal of helping to save the planet. As the club's English-language manual explains: "the primary function of the Seikatsu Club is not to sell but to buy" (*Seikatsu Club*, 1988). This means that the club uses its buying power to influence producers of primary products as well as the processors of such staples as cooking oil and soy sauce. The club offers only one size and variety of each of its own products, and will sell no products that are detrimental to the health of the members or to the environment. Such an initiative may prove difficult to transfer to this country until we have been forced by events to value cooperation more than competition. There appears to be nothing yet comparable in the U.S., where most cooperatives are viewed by their members as ways of getting cheaper food, and few have acquired enough economic clout to influence their suppliers.

Yet the popularity of farmers' markets around the country attests to the fact that some fraction of consumers does like to know who is growing its food; and the astonishing success of such "green" enterprises as the "Seventh Generation" and the "Body Shop" catalogues demonstrates that many consumers do wish to make their purchases count by buying environmentally responsible products. Can we lead them further than that? Over against all the barriers to public enlightenment that can lead to despair, we must put the infinite capacity of humans to grow and—even under the most unlikely circumstances—to change.

At the time of the oil crisis of the 1970s, there were convincing hints

Principles of the Seikatsu Club

What started as a strategy to save money gradually developed over the next 20 years into a philosophy encompassing "the whole of life. In addition to cost-effective collective purchase, the club is committed to a host of social concerns, including the environment, the empowerment of women and workers' conditions.

The primary function of the Seikatsu Club is not to sell but to buy. Unlike most Japanese co-ops which distribute merchandise through their stores, the club delivers goods directly to its members. Primary products like rice, milk, chicken, eggs, fish and vegetables make up 60 percent of our total stock. Seasonings such as miso and soy, processed foods and general merchandise like powdered soup, clothing and kitchen utensils are also available.

Membership Investment

In order to cope with rising competition with supermarkets and other cooperatives, many co-ops have sought to expand by decreasing investment and increasing dividends. But we believe that our business should be run by our own investments. This is part of the club's vision to reduce the division between producer, consumer and investor. When members join the co-op, they make an initial investment of 1,000 yen. This, supplemented by monthly contributions of 1,000 yen, brings the average investment to roughly 47,000 yen per person, which is returned whenever a member leaves the coop.

Our investment strategy has been highly successful: although the membership (153,000) ranks ninth out of Japan's 700 co-ops, for instance, we are fourth in terms of investment capital which totals 7.5 billion yen. Because the point of investment is not profit, the club does not offer dividends to its members.

Collective Buying

The Seikatsu Club utilizes a unique collective purchase system which relies on a) advance orders, b) distribution and payment based on a "han" or group, c) the concept of "one product/one variety," which limits the availability of any given item to a single brand.

When the club first got its start, we studied various co-op systems throughout Japan. Unable to find a method suitable to our needs, we developed our own original system: advance ordering. Once a month, members place orders one week before each purchase so that producers can plan in advance. This system also ensures freshness which means that preservatives are not necessary in our original brand food.

Individual members have no real buying power in the Seikatsu Club. A "han," composed of 6-13 families, is the basic unit for collective purchasing, and must buy in bulk—a minimum of 15 cartons of milk or seven kilograms of eggs, for instance. Items sold in bulk include pork, processed meat, frozen seafood and vegetables.

An autonomous local group which makes purchasing and broader policy decisions, the "han" has been useful in increasing pro-

Principles of the Seikatsu Club — continued

duction and distribution efficiency, reducing cost and promoting cooperative labor within the group. Through encouraging members to participate freely and actively and to train and educate each other, the club is also striving to nurture self-management skills.

Co-op staff delivers most goods in 1-1.5 ton trucks, while food requiring refrigeration is distributed by Taiyo Food Sales Co. Receipt and dispersal of merchandise and collection of orders, however, is handled by members. In the beginning of each month, order forms, catalogues and newsletters are distributed to "han" members by a member-on-duty. One week later, members pay for the previous month's order. The following week, advance orders are taken by another member-on-duty, and processed by computer using the OCR system. Milk deliveries, called "milk mail," are made twice a week. Eggs, pork, processed foods and seasonings are distributed once a week. All other goods, including rice, are distributed once a month.

"One Product/One Variety"

Although most coops offer a wide range of merchandise, the club handles only 400 products in total. We believe that limiting quantity ensures quality; as a result, we offer only one version of any given product. Soy sauce is produced in numerous sizes and shapes in Japan, but we provide nothing other than one liter glass bottles of thick soy. Through limiting variety, the club is able to streamline production and distribution. It also enables us to make special demands of producers—like leaving out preservatives.

The club also feels that limiting options cultivates creativity in daily life. We do not deal with salad dressing, for example, because we want to encourage members to make their own.

Respecting the Environment

We refuse to handle products if they are detrimental to the health of our members or the environment. Synthetic detergents, artificial seasoning and clothing made with fluorescents are all off limits, even if members make demands for them.

But our commitment to the environment is far more extensive than that. For one thing, the club gets safer produce by cooperating with local farmers. In return for asking them to use organic fertilizer and fewer chemicals, members buy a contracted amount of produce and agree to overlook physical imperfections if they exist. Members also assist farmers with the harvest when their labor is necessary.

We stand by the belief that housewives can begin to create a society that is harmonious with nature by "taking action from the home." And through our purchases and consumption, we are attempting to change the way that Japanese agriculture and fisheries are operated. As a symbolic gesture of societal responsibility for past crimes due to careless industrialization, we buy summer oranges from families with Minamata disease.

Principles of the Seikatsu Club — continued

When the club cannot find products which meet our quality, ecological or social standards, we will consider starting our own eneterprise. This can be illustrated by the two organic milk production facilities we currently run with local dairy farmers.

We also have an agreement with an organic agricultural co-op in the Shounai district of Yamagata prefecture: beginning with rice in 1972, it gradually expanded to vegetables and fruit, and now accounts for 30 percent of our total purchases.

Buying directly from producers does more than merely eliminate the middleman's added distribution cost. It enhances cooperation and awareness by keeping consumers in touch with the production process. That is why our annual summer excursion to Shounai, which has attracted more than 1,000 members since 1974, is so meaningful.

Source: The Seikatsu Club, Tokyo: Seikatsu Club Consumer Co-operative, 1988, pp. 6-8.

---

that as long as citizens believed that the suffering was shared and the shortage real (not merely a plot by the oil companies to force higher prices), they were willing to begin to adapt. Public education about limits—to energy first, and then to many of the other things energy is required for—seemed to be making progress in the mid-1970s until it became clear that the oil companies were indeed exaggerating the actual shortages for their own profit. At that point, the will to believe that supplies of everything were still unlimited snapped back into place—a reversion helped along, once the 1980s arrived, by the Reagan presidency.

But still-recent events in Eastern Europe have confirmed for us how little we know about large-scale social change. There will be innumerable wise men to tell us after the fact why the Cold War ended, but we would have looked for them in vain before it happened. When it comes to telling us what "they" will do tomorrow, it is clear that the social sciences have little to offer.

Will it take a further disaster to wake *us* up? It is certainly possible, although one would think that Chernobyl, the Exxon Valdez and the ongoing conflagration in the Amazon would be disasters enough to rouse us. Long before the summer of 1989 changed all our assumptions about the Cold War, I heard The Reverend William Sloan Coffin eloquently present the arguments as to why we did not need any land-based missiles at all—given our extensive sea and air based defenses—and how our buildup of nuclear arms was threatening the entire globe. After he finished speaking, someone in the audience asked him whether he really thought our country would change direction without a disaster. "I really don't know," he said. "But every morning I get up and pray for a small disaster."

It is possible that all of us concerned about the creation of a humane and sustainable food system ought to pray every morning—perhaps to Demeter, goddess of agriculture and social order, among other things—for a small and appropriate disaster, one that empowers the people to demand of their leaders evidence of their concern for the survival of the planet. Until the right disaster arrives, however, I feel obligated as an educator to think of what we can do now that will ultimately help people choose the route that leads away from Chicken Little. There are numerous educational tasks to be undertaken, and while some of them are directly related to the food system, only one of those will be ad-dressed—the relationships between price and food safety. We will then move on to where I believe the energies of those who understand the problem should be invested, namely, the broader environmental move-ment.

Will Fear Change the System?

The statistics that have most encouraged those who hoped that food safety fears would drive reform come from a 1988 pre-Alar survey that found 84.2 percent of Americans claiming they would buy organic food if it were available, and 49 percent expressing a willingness to pay higher prices for it (Howell, 1989; Whynott, 1989). We earlier com-mented on the limitations of the hope that consumers might be moved *beyond* fear of chemicals on their produce to an understanding of the larger issues affecting the food supply. It may turn out to be optimistic even to count on fear as a continuing motive.

If available surveys can be believed, interest in "natural" food may actually have declined. The Food Marketing Institute regularly surveys a national sample of consumers about their food supply concerns. The results demonstrate the vagaries of survey research *and* the extent to which consumer fear is a sometime thing. In January of 1990, 71 per-cent of consumers said "product safety" was a very important attribute of food, and when read a list of items "that may or may not constitute a health hazard" 80 percent identified "residues such as pesticides and herbicides" as a "serious hazard" and 56 percent so identified "anti-biotics and hormones in poultry and livestock." The first figure represented a slight increase over the seven years it has been asked (up from 77 percent); the latter figure represented a *decrease* (down from 61 percent).

When asked directly about the safety of the food supply, 79 percent of customers indicated that they were mostly or completely confident that the food in their supermarkets was safe. Less than 20 percent of shoppers listed pesticide residues and only 2 percent listed antibiotics in response to an open-ended question about "the greatest threats to the safety of the food you eat." Finally, when asked "what is it about the nutritional content of what you eat that concerns you and your family most?" the percentage that listed "as natural as possible" dropped from 12 percent in 1983 to 2 percent in 1990, while concern with avoiding "chemical additives" dropped from 27 percent to 4 percent over the same period (*FMI Trends,* 1990). A subsequent Louis Harris survey found a decline in the percentage of people willing to pay more for organic (Fabricant, 1990).

So rumors to the contrary notwithstanding, the public's anxiety over "chemicals" in the food supply may not be increasing, and it is hard to get nationally reliable data about their tendency to pay more for produce because they know it has been grown in a sustainable way. Figures on sales of "organic food" as a proportion of the annual food bill are too inconsistent to be useful. (If the percentage of U.S. farms that are organic is less than 2 percent—and most of these are small- to medium-sized—then the often-quoted claim that 3 percent of the annual food bill is "organic" seems improbable at best.) It is equally difficult to assess the continuing demand for organic produce since a substantial fraction does not flow through conventional channels.

In a recent issue of the journal *Contemporary Policy Issues,* the authors of an article on "Organic Food and Sustainable Agriculture" make the point that without a national legal definition of the term organic "some consumers may be confusing *chemical-free* with *organically grown* and paying a premium for the perception that a change in farming practices has occurred" (Hall, et al, 1989). The authors seem to be assuming that significant numbers of consumers understand that there is something beyond "pesticide-free" which they *ought* to be paying for, although at the moment it is not at all certain that many consumers make such distinctions.

Moreover, many people in the organic movement believe that "no pesticides" is a questionable selling point for organic because a truly sustainable agriculture may not be entirely "free of chemicals." Earth's Best, a highly successful organic baby food company, discovered just how dangerous a "no pesticides" standard could be when a story hit the press claiming that New York State's Department of Agriculture and Markets had found a pesticide residue in some jars of their sweet potato. Although the residue was well under allowable levels and the real dispute was over labeling, the incident has heightened awareness in the organic/sustainable community of the riskiness of focusing on residues (Mann and Yarrow, 1990).

Organic producers themselves realize, however, that much of the buying public is presently willing to pay more for organic not because it is better for the environment but because it promises to be freer of pesticide residues. In an editorial in the second issue of a new publication called *Organic Farmer,* editor Grace Gershuny points out:

> The time is right for organic farmers to emphasize the ethical, humane components of our approach. Our products are "hot" largely because of health concerns right now.... We must make it clear that what we advocate is a radical departure from a food system built on exploitation—of the soil, or animals, and of other human beings. As corporate America and the Federal government latch onto organic farming, we have to publicly proclaim that our solutions are not just technological but moral ones (Gershuny, 1990).

But whether the public is willing to pay for morality in agriculture, or merely for purity in their food, leading them to a real understanding of farming and sustainability will require confronting the problem of cost. Consumers who wish to help create a truly sustainable food system may need to be willing to spend more for food and drink than the 11 to 16 percent it now takes out of their budgets (Ambry, 1990). In relation to incomes, U.S. food is cheap, probably too cheap (although in terms of the nation's total demand on natural resources, Americans now eat expensively, as the sidebar on page 108 shows). High animal protein consumption puts diets of most Americans out of reach of the majority of the world's people.

It is easy to say, as those of us concerned with this issue tend to, that if all the costs of our present sort of farming were counted, organic food would be cheaper. At this point it is not, and asking people to pay more for food is always a politically difficult thing to do. Although most Americans pay considerably less for food as a percentage of their incomes than other people in the world, they are likely to turn out of office any administration that proposes that it cost more. Sometime during the course of the Carter administration, there was a rumor afloat that the President, in his hoped-for second term, planned to let the price of California water rise to its true cost. This free-market gesture was breathtaking. For if California water were allowed to cost what it was *worth*—even by present accounting methods, even discounting its long-term value—the cost of California produce would rise dramatically. To allow the cost of California produce rise was to stimulate agriculture elsewhere, which had been undercut by the astonishing effect of lavishing unlimited, essentially free water on the deserts of California.

If Carter had won a second term and acted on the rumor as forecast, it would have been political dynamite, as the price of food would immediately have risen. Even a communicator more skilled than President Carter would have had a hard time explaining to an American public, nibbled to dullness by television sound-bytes, the positive, long-term effects of such a move. In the long run the relocalization of agriculture would have helped revive farming communities across the country; it might have actually lowered the relative price of food, once the transportation and other costs of centralized industrial agriculture began to show up in the price of the food it produced. But in the short run raising the price of California water would have raised food costs to the consumer. And in America it is the short run that counts in business and in politics.

To counter any such "higher costs" scenario, corporate agribusiness can offer the public a collection of products, heavily advertised as tasty, convenient *and* healthy in which the actual *food* represents a mere 7 to 10 percent of the companies' costs so that "any big rise in raw material prices can be covered by a relatively small increase in the price of packaged food" (Krebs, 1989). Not only that—the companies who will make these foods are big and powerful and understand the not-so-gentle arts of persuasion. Former Federal Trade Comission Chairman Michael Pertshuk was only half jesting when he predicted that "by the year 2000 there will be two consumer goods companies in the United States: RJR Nabisco will be selling all the consumer goods west of the Mississippi, and Philip Morris will be selling all the consumer goods east of the Mississippi" (Krebs, 1989). The new Philip Morris magazine, replete with lively copy, color photos and a variety of ads—all for the company's products—reminds us how far along the road we have been taken.

Against this, advocates of a sustainable food system offer a much more complex package which must be sold to the public without the assistance of the financial resources Philip Morris commands. But that cannot be helped. If food must become more expensive, consumers will

The Real Cost of Our "Cheap" Food

Source: "The Politics of Food Trade" by Kevin Danaher
(Paper presented at The Other Economic
Summit (TOES) 1988, Toronto)

[C]oncentration of control in the food system is an acceptable price to pay, we are told, because the American people are getting cheap food. But is our food really cheap?

The problem with the "cheap" food argument is that it is based on a misunderstanding of real costs. First, farmers' income is a very small portion of the price the consumer pays for food in the store: there are only a few pennies worth of wheat in a box of Wheaties, for example. The bulk of the price goes to the large corporations that dominate the provision of farm inputs, and the shipping, processing, advertising, wholesaling and retailing of the product. So raising farm prices would not necessarily cost as much as many consumers have been led to believe.

Second, "cheap" food refers only to *money price,* not the total cost—socially and environmentally—of the current food system. The environmental costs of industrial agriculture can fill volumes, so we will only hint at the dimensions of the problem with a few facts. The National Academy of Sciences estimates that pesticide residues in food cause 20,000 cancer deaths every year. American farms lose some 2 billion tons of topsoil per year, resulting in lost productivity estimated at somewhere between $1 billion and $43 billion each year. This is not a *sustainable* system of agriculture. The big push to export has accelerated the process of natural resource depletion and pollution due

to increased pressure to produce more product from limited acreage.

The economic dynamics behind these environmental costs can be seen in a specific example.

Ed Hauck was an award-winning conservation farmer in Wabaska County, Minnesota. He bought a badly eroded farm in 1958 and restored it to model condition with terraces, strip cropping, waterways and contour farming. By 1984, Hauck had cut soil erosion to less than 3 tons per acre per year.

But Hauck's farm was foreclosed by John Hancock Insurance Company. The company rented the farm to a tenant who sought to increase output by plowing up the entire farm. Hauck's decades of conservation work were destroyed in a few years. The annual soil loss is now estimated at 35-40 tons per acre.

Third, the human costs to low-paid farmworkers and dispossessed farmers are reflected in terrible working conditions and high suicide rates. Unemployment among farmers and farmworkers has soared over the past decade. Farmers leaving the land crowd into cities and put downward pressure on wage rates.

Cheap food translates into keeping the wage bill down for employers, while making life more competitive for farmers and workers. Displaced farmers and their families pay less taxes and often become dependent on government social services, including food stamps. By knocking family farmers out of busi-

---

The Real Cost of Our "Cheap" Food — continued

ness, our food system increasingly concentrates control of land in the hands of fewer owners, thus undermining the democratic values we claim to hold dear.

Finally, there are hidden financial costs to this allegedly cheap food. In 1986, U.S. taxpayers paid out $26 billion in farm subsidies—more than $433 per family of four—mainly to the biggest, richest farmers.

A key reason for the much-touted "efficiency" of industrial agriculture is that these many costs are not paid by agribusiness, but are instead absorbed by the general public. Even the key measure of national production, the Gross National Product, mystifies the entire production process by failing to subtract these costs from total output, instead counting most of them positively as contributions to the total.

---

need to understand the reasons why and be willing to pay the price. Four years ago, reviewing a book on the international infant formula campaign, the *New Internationalist* observed that the book carried two messages: "the first is that multinationals are not invincible," and the second "that an informal and tenacious international network of like-minded people can shift corporate and government policy" (*New Internationalist,* 1986).

Who is to make up such a "tenacious international network of like-minded people" where the reform of the food system is involved? Who is there who can stand up to the concentrated corporate power? The understanding that has come to me only in the course of writing this book is that it may not be possible to begin by urging eaters toward the "solution" of a more local and less processed food supply. To suggest that people change what they eat for conscious political reasons is to raise all the emotional associations that "my" foods evoke—and to find oneself trying to lead a band of reluctant followers through the rapids of confusion about health, safety and long-term sustainability in the food system.

But to speak to people as concerned citizens, whose eco-system is being permanently despoiled, is to tap into an urgent concern that literally millions of people are presently acting on—as members of local citizens committees, as contributors to national environmental groups or both. Some of the best work done on the environmental issues today is being done by local groups, fired by local grievances. A potent symbol of such local activism is "ordinary housewife" Lois Gibbs, who be-

BIZARRO   By DAN PIRARO

The BIZARRO cartoon is reprinted by permission of Chronicle Features, San Francisco, California.

came a citizen activist over the toxic wastes buried in Love Canal.

A new relocalization of the environmental movement is presently under way. But at the moment, local environmentalists are seldom involved in saving local farmland as farmland. Indeed, in my own community, when a commission was set up to look at local planning/environmental issues for the year 2000, one of the early suggestions in regard to our rapidly declining farmland was that we should buy five acres or so of one of the remaining farms as a sort of museum "so our children can see how food *used to be* produced." Nor is my county unique in contemplating a farm theme park (Egan, 1989). Those of us concerned about maintaining local food-producing capacity, about creating such local economies as those Wendell Berry describes in the sidebar on the opposite page, must get our local environmental groups

Source: Wendell Berry, *What Are People For?*

Two facts are immediately apparent. One is that the present local economy, based like the economies of most rural places exclusively on the export of raw materials, is ruinous. Another is that the influence of a complex, aggressive national economy upon a simple, passive local economy will also be ruinous. In a varied and versatile countryside, fragile in its composition and extremely susceptible to abuse, requiring close human care and elaborate human skills, able to produce and needing to produce a great variety of products from its soils, what is needed, obviously, is a highly diversified local economy.

We should be producing the fullest variety of foods to be consumed locally, in the countryside itself and in nearby towns and cities: meats, grains, table vegetables, fruits and nuts, dairy products, poultry and eggs. We should be harvesting a sustainable yield of fish from our ponds and streams. Our woodlands, managed for continuous yields, selectively and carefully logged, should be yielding a variety of timber for a variety of purposes: firewood, fence posts, lumber for building, fine woods for funiture makers.

And we should be adding value locally to these local products. What is needed is not the large factory so dear to the hearts of government "developers." To set our whole population to making computers or automobiles would be as gross an error as to use the whole countryside for growing corn or Christmas trees or pulpwood; it would discount everything we have to offer as a community and a place; it would despise our talents and capacities as individuals.

We need, instead, a system of decentralized, small-scale industries to transform the products of our fields and woodlands and streams: small creameries, cheese factories, canneries, grain mills, saw mills, furniture factories, and the like. By "small" I mean simply a size that would not be destructive of the appearance, the health, and the quiet of the countryside. If a factory began to "grow" or to be noisy at night or on Sunday, that would mean that another such factory was needed somewhere else. If waste should occur at any point, that would indicate the need for an enterprise of some other sort. If poison or pollution resulted from any enterprise, that would be understood as an indication that something was absolutely wrong, and a correction would be made. Small scale, of course, makes such changes and corrections more thinkable and more possible than does large scale.

I realize that, by now, my argument has crossed a boundary line of which everyone in our "realistic" society is keenly aware. I will be perceived to have crossed over into "utopianism" or fantasy. Unless I take measures to prevent it, I am going to hear somebody say, "All that would be very nice, if it were possible. Can't you be realistic?"

Well, let me take measures to prevent it. I am not, I admit, optimistic about the success of this kind of thought. Otherwise, my intention, above all, is to be realistic; I wish to be practical. The question here is simply that of convention. Do I want to be realistic according to the conventions of the industrial economy and the military state, or according to what I know of reality? To me, an economy that sees the life of a community or a place as expendable, and reckons its value only in terms of money, is not acceptable because it is *not* realistic. I am thinking as I believe we must think if we wish to discuss the *best* uses of people, places, and things, and if we wish to give affection some standing in our thoughts.

by the throat to explain that environmental quality is a product of active and self-reliant local communities and that a community's capacity to produce some of its own food is one basis for local self-reliance (Berry, 1989).

Indeed, it is becoming increasingly clear that unless environmental groups begin to incorporate farmland into their definition of "natural places worth saving," the urgencies of those who can find no other land on which to produce food will inevitably help ravage the wild places environmentalists are now working to protect around the world.

Yes, But What Can I Do Now?

Whether one approaches responsible eating as a food-aware environmentalist or an ecologically aware eater, there will always come a point when specific decisions have to be made in the marketplace. People who are already concerned want to make responsible choices now. It is at this point that one becomes aware of how obscured the connections are between the foods one acquires and the viability of local agriculture. A number of researchers have attempted to determine how consumers' actions and intentions in regard to food purchasing may reflect their environmental concern, or lack of it, for food system sustainability. But once one moves beyond trying to buy locally, seasonally or organically grown—whatever one cannot personally produce—really informed choices are hard to make.

To begin with, as we have noted earlier, ownership of corporations is increasingly concentrated—with, as one consumer put it, "cigarette companies and food and chemical companies and dealers with South Africa" all mixed up together (*The Shopper Report,* 1990). And once one has decided—perhaps with the help of the Council on Economic Priorities' booklet *Shopping for a Better World*—which companies to deal with at all, hard questions remain. In this store, at this time and in this community is it better to buy recyclable glass or plastic bottles? And, assuming you opt not to make your own—and I do not—is it better to buy local non-organic fresh tortillas or frozen organic ones that have traveled 2,000 miles?

In this regard the Green Consuming movement may be a help. A number of environmental groups are now trying to sort out for the rest of us what is truly "green" and what is merely "consuming" among the rash of "natural," recyclable" and "biodegradable" products in the supermarket. Such help is essential. For while local activists can best save local farms and communities, "all the local efforts in the world will ultimately be insignificant if the corporate commercial juggernaut continues unchecked, to waste the lion's share of the nation's savings, resources, and labor on the production of an induced consumption of superfluity" (Clark 1989).

Thus, sorting out the choices is challenging but also—and I use this word advisedly—fun. I am inspired to use this particular word by a marvelous interview by Jason DeParle of the *New York Times* with Ralph Nader, that paragon of civic virtue who has been variously characterized, according to the *Times* article, as "shrill, dour and a national nag." The interviewer commented that while most people entered the public sphere to produce better schools or fewer toxic wastes, Mr. Nader seemed to view public services as an end in itself. "I just think that striving for justice, when you spell it out, has to be seen as a source of pleasure," he is quoted as saying (DeParle, 1990). And that is where it comes out. Eating responsibly is more fun than eating any other way; the choices offered are by far the most interesting, the most frequent and in many ways the most important choices one gets to make, since they can contribute not only to the health of oneself but of the earth.

Realism and Hope

Presumably, the task of this chapter was to show how we can get from where we are now to the kind of sustainable food system many of us believe to be essential if the human race is to survive the 21st century—a food system that is something like the one Wendell Berry describes in the sidebar. And as I have come to realize, the reason why the concluding section of this essay has been so difficult to write is that I simply don't know how we will get to where many of us think we ought to be in the century that begins in less than 10 years.

So while this chapter is intended to be about hope, it is not, alas, about solutions. That is why—despite evidence that fragments of the system are beginning to shift in the SHE direction—analysis compels me to admit that the forces driving toward more concentration, more artifice, more manipulations of (rather than cooperation with) nature seem all but overwhelming. This is why I have concluded that the task for those of us who wish to save real food is to reach the public through their existing environmental concerns, which they can utlimately connect to their personal behavior and specifically to their choices of food.

And I have written this book at least partly because I worry that the

How giving up nest eggs made more jobs

Today a lot of people are working because a man who made medicated nest eggs had an eager, restless mind.

Orator F. Woolward was the man and it was in Le Roy, N. Y. before the turn of the century. He was doing well with the nest egg business—but not well enough. Hens were appreciative but farmers took a heap of selling.

So he went into the food business with a coffee substitute. This went well—well enough that he began thinking about branching out and finally became interested in a gelatin dessert which had been perfected by a local builder named Wait.

The dessert idea was only a side line with Mr. Wait. Because he wanted to keep on being a carpenter, he sold Mr. Woodward the rights and trade-mark— and the trade-mark was JELL-O!

At first, sales came hard—so hard that Mr. Woodward once offered to **sell the whole JELL-O business for $30** and there were no takers! But year by year the business began to pick up.

As the JELL-O business grew, it made more and more jobs for more and more people. Jobs and work—not only for those who made JELL-O—but for shippers and warehousemen, for distributors and grocers. It benefited farmers. too . . . for good prices on farm products depend on people having jobs and being able to pay good money for good food.

Today, everyone agrees that America faces a serious problem in postwar employment. There must be steady jobs by the millions.

Most people want these jobs made the way Woodward did it—in the typical American way. Through expansion of existing businesses, through new business enterprises, large or small. Through initiative and ingenuity in making new products, better products like JELL-O, or giving some better service.

There is no equivalent for this American way of making jobs. It has made this nation the most prosperous of all nations. It has given Americans the highest stand-ard of living in the world. And it has made agriculture in America more profitable than in any other country.

The freedom that has made this possible—freedom to start a business, expand a business or hang out your own shingle—is not a freedom to be taken lightly, or for granted. Americans want it, Americans need it, for making jobs and building prosperity in the peacetime future.

Hence, it is a freedom to be fostered and advanced by all Americans, including yourself.

For you are a part of the public. Your opinion is part of public opinion. And public opinion is what shapes a country's destiny . . . _sets the pattern of its people's lives . . . determines what freedoms they_ may enjoy.

You owe it to yourself to be aware of this at all times. To let _your_ voice be heard and _your_ opinion be known on how you want jobs to be made in _your_ country.

JELL-O IS A PRODUCT OF GENERAL FOODS AND AMERICAN ENTERPRISE people most committed to working for a truly sustainable food system are simply not in touch with the TV-driven, artifice-filled supermarket world in which most consumers make their food choices. A new friend of mine, a gifted and passionate organic farmer with whom I was contemplating a project, served me fried parsnips with syrup for breakfast one morning and said with excitement, "See, Joan, all we have to do is let people know that all this delicious food is out there—let them know that it's all available—and they'll eat it up!" "You don't understand," I replied, "what they're eating now is pop-tarts." What I should have added was that the next generation whom we are counting on to save us are learning that shelf-stable microwavable dinners can be bought off the shelf at Toys-'R'-Us.

When even Jell-O seems to the harried and deskilled contemporary homemaker "too complicated" to make for desert, the problems facing those of us who wish to change the food system are clearly not food problems, but value problems. Eating Jell-O will not help the farmer now any more than a half-century ago when General Foods claimed it would (see pages 103-104). And neither will eating pop-tarts or using microwave popcorn—even organic microwave popcorn. But people who have been taught only to consume, believing that all production is to be avoided as drudgery, will be difficult to entice back to the joys of a greater involvement in their own food supply.

Although it is not at all clear from the data that people have less free time than they used to—working moms notwithstanding—people *believe* they have less time and marketers are selling to the perception that watching "Thirtysomething" is a better thing to do than prepare a meal from raw food materials (Robinson, 1990).

In the end, what it comes down to is how much people can really be made to care about *themselves*. When The Other Economic Summit (TOES) met in Toronto in 1988, one of the speakers, Rod Shouldice, was the leader of the Community Supported Agriculture movement described in this chapter. He began his speech as follows: "Someone out there is growing you." And that, finally, is the point. Someone is going to produce and subsequently manipulate the materials out of which each of us is made. Are people really prepared to trust that responsibility to Philip Morris?

Epilogue: In the Garden . . . Again

It turns out that something other than larval wilt may have done in our gypsy moth caterpillars this past year. A couple of Dartmouth scientists discovered that the leaves of oaks that have been devoured one year are replaced in following years by leaves that are drier, tougher and higher in growth-retarding tannins—that are, in short, just a lot less tasty and nutritious for gypsy moth larvae (Schultz and Baldwin, 1982). So our trees apparently have a hand in their own protection. Will wonders never cease!

I, for one, hope not. We cannot afford to be without wonders. As we make our peace with nature, it begins to look as if she will always show herself more subtle, more surprising, more self-controlled, more full of wonder than we ourselves can ever hope to be.

There are some things I would enjoy understanding though. For example, why do Daddy-long-legs like potato vines so much, consistently year after year? I assume they find something to eat there, which I am happy to let them have. There are no potato bugs at all, but it is hard to tell whether we ought to give credit to the Daddy-long-legs, the beans we interplanted or simply to the cool wet weather that appears to have discouraged some of the *plants* as well. Other possibilities exist. I was out the other day checking the potatoes for striped cucumber beetles—which appear to like everything in the garden—when something red caught my eye. A potato beetle larva, I thought, as I reached out to squash it. But I stopped in time; it was a friend—one of those tiny triangular dragons that grow up to be. ladybugs. A similar case of mistaken identity had tripped me up a couple of days earlier when I saw what I thought was a young katydid and suddenly realized that it was a

117

tender green young mantis—not substantial enough yet to prey on a large scale, but doubtless out stalking aphids.

The complexity of the garden is simply overwhelming—the small wasps come year after year to hover around the broccoli. I was always certain they were helping discourage something, but I could not figure out what until the day I saw one carrying off a limp cabbage moth larvae bigger than itself. I doubt that the whole system is really "solvable," although I keep notes in the hope that someday it will all hang together and that one year I will be *certain* that the cantaloupe is aphid-free because of the marigolds and not because of the nasturtiums and onions— or simply because we grew tomatoes in that spot last year. I am not willing to simplify in order to solve it, however, The complexity is much too productive.

Spraying would simplify it all, but the price is too high. With patience, by making careful observations and minimal interventions, producers at every scale can learn to distinguish friends from enemies, can even learn that some potential enemies left alone will do no real harm. The alternative, unfortunately, is simply an accelerated destruction of essential diversity.

A friend mentioned to me not long ago a conversation she had had with a young woman working in what is called IPM or integrated pest management. This is an approach to the control of economically harmful pests by holding back to let nature handle as much of the job as possible, and then intervening minimally and only when the alternative is serious crop loss. My friend said that this was the first year that she had gotten out there and squashed the potato beetles by hand, picking the eggs off the bottoms of the leaves. She said that she had remarked to the IPM advocate that it was so much cleaner to get out there and spray with Sevin. "You're right," the IPM woman replied. "Pinching is messy. It's a little like having to defend yourself in hand-to-hand combat. Launching a missile is much simpler."

Bibliography for Chapters 1-7

Ambry, Margaret, The Age of Spending. *American Demographics* 12(11), November 1990, p. 18.

American Chemical Society. (Information pamphlet: *Pesticides*). Washington, DC: American Chemical Society, n.d.

Anderson, Walter Truett. Food Without Farms. *The Futurist;* January/February 1990, pp. 16-21.

Ansilomar Declaration for Sustainable Agriculture, The. (Ecological Farming Conference). Pacific Grove, CA: Ansilomar Conference Center, January 12, 1990, 2-page mimeo.

Antosh, Nelson. *Houston Chronicle,* December 10, 1989.

Baum, Hilary. Public Markets Collaborative. Personal communication, 1991.

Baumel, C. Phillip and Marvin Hayenga. Domestic Food Security: Transportation and Marketing Issues. In: Busch and Lacy, eds., *Food Security, op cit.*

Belasco, Warren. *Appetite for Change: How the Counterculture Took on the Food Industry, 1966-1988.* New York: Pantheon Books, 1989.

Benedick, Richard Elliot. Ecological Diplomacy: An Agenda for 1990. *Scientific American,* January 1990, p. 154.

Berry, Wendell. *What Are People For?* San Francisco: North Point Press, 1990.

Billard, J.B. The Revolution in American Agriculture. *National Geographic* 137, February 1970, pp. 147-185.

Black, Gail. Organic Livestock: Humane Alternatives. *Organic Farmer* 1(2), Spring 1990, pp. 9-11.

Block to Serve as Farm Spokesman. *Nutrition Week,* January 1, 1981, p. 8.

Bock, Gregory and Joan Marsh, eds. *Applications of Plant Cell and Tissue Culture.* Ciba Foundation Symposium No. 137. New York: John Wiley, 1988.

Bray, Garth. Disney Zoo Kills Birds. *Multinational Monitor,* November 1989, p. 32.

Brody, Jane. Outwitting Nature to Produce More Food. *New York Times,* January 23, 1980.

_____. New Index Finds Some Cancer Dangers Are Overrated and Others Ignored. *New York Times.* April 17, 1987a.

_____. Personal Health: An Index to Put the Risk of Cancer in Perspective. *New York Times,* April 12, 1987b.

_____. Personal Health: Sorting Out Data on Diet and Cancer. *New York Times,* September 30, 1987c, pp. C-1, C-8.

Brooks, Harvey. Can Science Survive in the Modern Age? *Science* 174, October 1, 1971, pp. 21-30.

Brooks, Nancy Rivera and Tom Furlong. Expensive Victory for Business. *Los Angeles Times,* November 9, 1990, pp. D-1, D-5.

Brown, Mark Malloch, ed. *Famine: A Man-Made Disaster.* A Report for the Independent Commission on International Humanitarian Issues. London: Pan Books, 1985.

Busch, Lawrence. Biotechnology: Consumer Concerns About Risks and Values. *Food Technology* 45(4), April 1991, pp. 96-101.

Busch, Lawrence and William B. Lacy, eds. *Food Security in the United States,* Boulder, CO: Westview Press, 1984.

Busch, Lawrence, William B. Lacy, Jeffrey Burkhardt and Laura R. Lacy. *Plants, Power and Profit: Social, Economic and Ethical Consequences of the New Biotechnology.* Oxford: Blackwell, 1991.

Carper, Jean. *The Food Pharmacy.* New York: Bantam Books, 1988.

Charlier, Marj. 'Organic' May Soon Be Easier to Swallow. *Wall Street Journal,* November 28, 1990, pp. B-1, B-8.

Clark, Richard. Response to Richard Conlin's Critique of the Addicted Society in *Human Economy Newsletter* 10(4), December 1989, pp.

8-10.

Coleman, Eliot. *The New Organic Grower*. Chelsea, VT: Chelsea Green, 1989.

Companies Can Capitalize on Healthful Implications of Certain Foods Says Arthur D. Little Nutritionist (News Release). Cambridge, MA: Arthur D. Little, September 1, 1988.

Cornucopia Project, The. *Empty Breadbasket? The Coming Challenge to America's Food Supply and What We Can Do About It*. Emmaus, PA: Cornucopia Project of Rodale Press, 1981.

Council on Economic Priorities (CEP), *Shopping for a Better World*. New York: CEP, 1991.

Crosson, Pierre. What Is Alternative Agriculture? *American Journal of Alternative Agriculture* 4(1), 1989, pp. 28-31.

Dahlberg, Kenneth. *Beyond the Green Revolution*. New York: Plenum Press, 1979.

Dando, William. *The Geography of Famine*. New York: John Wiley, 1980.

DeParle, Jason. Eclipsed in the Reagan Decade, Ralph Nader Again Feels Glare of the Public. *New York Times*, September 21, 1990.

Doyle, Jack. *Altered Harvest: Agriculture, Genetics and the Fate of the World's Food Supply*. New York: Viking Penguin, 1985.

Dupont, H. L. Consumption of Raw Shellfish—Is the Risk Now Unacceptable? *New England Journal of Medicine* 314, March 13, 1986, p. 707.

Durning, Alan. Breadlines and Billionaires. *WorldWatch* 3(3), May/June 1990, p. 2.

Dziezak, Judie D. Biotechnology and Flavor Development: Plant Tissue Cultures. *Food Technology* 40(4), April 1986, pp. 122-129.

Edwards, Clive A. The Concept of Integrated Systems in Lower Input/Sustainable Agriculture. *American Journal of Alternative Agriculture* 2(4), Fall 1987.

Edwards, D.D. Alcohol-Breast Cancer Link. *Science News* 131, May 9, 1987, p. 292.

Egan, Timothy. Skagit Journal. Farmers Fear a Plague of Tourists with Park. *New York Times*, December 1989.

Ehrlich, Paul R. Environmental Disruption: Implications for the Social

Sciences. *Social Science Quarterly* 62, March 1981, pp. 7-22.

_____. The Limits to Substitution: Meta-resource Depletion and a New Economic-ecological Paradigm. *Ecological Economics* 1, 1989, pp. 9-16.

Elkin, A.P. Art and Life. In: Ronald M. Berndt, ed. *Australian Aboriginal Art*. New York: Macmillan, 1964.

Enshayan, Kamyar. Outlines, Complexity, and Breadth of Sustainability. Letter to *American Journal of Alternative Agriculture* 5(1), 1990, pp. 46-47.

Fabricant, Florence. The Bloom Off Organic Sales. *New York Times,* September 12, 1990.

Farm Bill 1990: Agenda for the Environment and Consumers. Washington, DC and Covelo, CA: Island Press, 1990, 24 pp.

Farmers' Markets: Good for Growers, Shoppers and Cities. *New York Times,* October 3, 1990.

Ferrando, R. *Traditional and Non-traditional Foods*. Rome: FAO, 1981.

Fisher, Lawrence M. A Tomato for the Ages? *New York Times,* October 7, 1990.

FMI Trends: Consumer Attitudes and the Supermarket, 1990. Washington, DC: Food Marketing Institute, 1990.

Food and Nutrition Board, Commission on Life Sciences, National Research Council. *Biotechnology and the Food Supply.* (Proceedings of a symposium). Washington, DC: National Academy Press, 1988.

Gazette. Texas Department of Agriculture, February 1990.

George, Susan. *How the Other Half Dies*. Montclair, NJ: Allanheld, Osmun, 1977.

_____. *A Fate Worse Than Debt*. New York: Grove Weidenfeld, 1990.

Gershuny, Grace. Editorial in *Organic Farmer* 1(2), Spring 1990, p. 6.

Gever, John, Robert Kaufmann, David Skole and Charles Vorosmarty. *Beyond Oil. The Threat to Food and Fuel in the Coming Decades.* Cambridge, MA: Ballinger, 1986.

Goldberg, Rebecca, Jane Rissler, Hope Shand and Chuck Hassebrook. *Biotechnology's Bitter Harvest: Herbicide-tolerate Crops and the*

Threat to Sustainable Agriculture. Report of the Biotechnology Working Group, March 1990. (Available from the Environmental Defense Fund, New York, NY, and the National Wildlife Federation, Washington, DC.)

Gore, Albert, Jr. The Gene Revolution. In: Food and Nutrition Board, *op cit.*

Green Book, The: A Directory of Wholesale Growers of Massachusetts Grown and Fresh Products. Boston: Bureau of Markets, Massachusetts Department of Food and Agriculture, 1990.

Greenwald, John. $25,000,000,000. *Time,* December 12, 1988, pp. 56-57.

Groh, Trauger M. and Steven S. H. McFadden. *Farms of Tomorrow. Community-supported Farms; Farm-supported Communities.* Kimberton, PA: Bio-Dynamic Farming and Gardening Association, 1990.

Guither, Harold. Developing Policy for a Resource-conserving Agriculture: The 1985 Food Security Act in Perspective. *American Journal of Alternative Agriculture* 1(1), Winter 1987.

Gussow, Alan. *A Sense of Place: The Artist and the American Land.* San Francisco: Friends of the Earth, 1972.

Gussow, Joan Dye. *The Feeding Web: Issues in Nutritional Ecology.* Palo Alto: Bull Publishing, 1978, Chapter 2.

_____. PCBs for Breakfast and Other Problems with a Food System Gone Awry. *Food Monitor,* May/June 1982, pp. 16-19 +28.

_____. A Modest Proposal. *Food Monitor* 2(3), Summer 1985, pp. 8-9.

Hackett, Thomas. Fire. *The New Yorker,* October 2, 1989, pp. 50-71.

Hall, Bob. Perdue Farms: Poultry and Profits. *Multinational Monitor,* September 1989, pp. 18-20.

Hall, Darwin C., Brian P. Baker, Jacques Franco and Desmond A. Jolly. Organic Food and Sustainable Agriculture. *Contemporary Policy Issues* 7, October 1989, pp. 47-72.

Hamel, Ruth. Living in Traffic. *American Demographics,* March 1989, pp. 49-51.

Hard to Swallow. *Multinational Monitor.* October, 1989, p. 30.

Hardin, Garrett. *Filters Against Folly: How to Survive Despite*

Ecologists, Economists, and the Merely Eloquent. New York: Viking, 1985.

Harley, J. L. and R. Scott Russell, eds. *The Soil-Root Interface: Proceedings of a Symposium.* New York: Academic Press, 1979.

Health and Environment Network. Nitrate: Rerun of an Old Horror. *Health and Environment Digest* 1(12), January 1988.

Healthy Harvest III: A Directory of Sustainable Agriculture & Horticulture Organizations, 1989-1990. (Deborah Preston, ed.). Washington, DC: Potomac Valley Press, 1989 (Suite 105, 1424 16th Street, NW, Washington, DC 20036).

Henderson, Hazel. Decision Making in the Solar Age. In: H. Nash, ed. *Progress as If Survival Mattered.* San Francisco: Friends of the Earth, 1981, pp. 48-61.

Herrin, Marcia and Joan D. Gussow. Designing a Sustainable Regional Diet. *Journal of Nutrition Education* 21(6), December 1989, pp. 270-275.

Holt, Donald A. Computers in Production Agriculture. *Science* 228, April 26, 1985, pp. 422-427.

How Safe Is Your Food? *Newsweek,* March 27, 1989.

Howell, Dan. Pesticide Scares: States Battle Food Fears. *Government News* 32(9), September 1989, pp. 7-9.

IFT Office of Scientific Public Affairs. Assessing the Optimal System for Ensuring Food Safety: A Scientific Consensus, August 29-30, 1988. Chicago: IFT, April 5, 1989, 25-page mimeo.

Ilker, Reinfriede. In-vitro Pigment Production: An Alternative to Color Synthesis. *Food Technology,* April 1987, pp. 70-72.

In the Dumpster. *Garbage* 1(1), 1989.

Is Anything Safe? *Time,* March 27, 1989.

Jackson, Wes, Wendell Berry and Bruce Colman, eds. *Meeting the Expectations of the Land.* San Francisco: North Point Press, 1984.

Kates, Robert. Excerpt from address to National Academy of Sciences Symposium on Hazards: Technology and Fairness. *NRC News Report,* July 1985.

Klausner, A. Researchers Cotton to New Fiber Findings. *Bio/Technology* 3(12), 1985, p. 1049.

Kneen, Brewster. Who Writes This Stuff Anyway? *The Ram's Horn,*

No. 67, November 1989.

Knorr, Dietrich. Food Biotechnology: Its Organization and Potential. *Food Technology,* April 1987, pp. 95-100.

Knorr, Dietrich and Anthony J. Sinskey. Biotechnology in Food Production and Processing. *Science* 229, September 30, 1985, pp. 1224-1229.

Kramer, Mark, *Three Farms: Making Milk, Meat and Money from the American Soil.* Boston and Toronto: Little, Brown, 1977.

Krebs, A.V. The Cost of Concentration: Monopolization in the Food Industry. *Multinational Monitor,* March 1989, pp. 13-17.

Lappé, Frances Moore. *Diet for a Small Planet.* New York: Ballantine Books, 1971.

Lappé, Frances Moore and Joseph Collins. *Food First.* Boston: Houghton Mifflin, 1977.

Leiss, William. *The Limits to Satisfaction: An Essay on the Problem of Needs and Commodities.* Toronto: University of Toronto Press, 1976, p. 38.

LISA Funding. *Alternative Agriculture News* 8(10), October 1990, p. 3.

Little, Arthur D. Implications for Food Processors. Chapter 3 in *Outlook for Food and Agribusiness* (Service to Management Series). Cambridge, MA: Arthur D. Little, May 1974.

Lockeretz, William. Open Questions in Sustainable Agriculture. *American Journal of Alternative Agriculture* 3(4), Fall 1988, pp. 174-181.

Lovins, Amory B. and L. Hunter Lovins. *Brittle Power.* Andover, MA: Brickhouse Publishing, 1982.

Lovins, Amory B., L. Hunter Lovins and Marty Bender. Energy and Agriculture. In: Jackson, Berry and Colman, eds., *Meeting the Expectations, op. cit.*

Lund, Daryl. Modified Foods Carry Industry into New Era. *Prepared Foods,* March 1987, p. 147.

Madden, Patrick. Can Sustainable Agriculture Be Profitable? *Environment* 29(4), 1987.

_____. Policy Options for a More Sustainable Agriculture. In: Farm Foundation, comp. *Increasing Understanding of Public*

Problems and Policies—1988. (Papers from National Public Policy Education Conference, Fall 1988). Oak Brook, IL: The Foundation, 1988, pp. 134-142.

_____. What Is Alternative Agriculture? *American Journal of Alternative Agriculture* 4(1), 1989, pp. 32-34.

Make Everything 'Natural' Through Biotechnology: Hall. *Food Chemical News,* April 2, 1990, p. 62.

Mann, John David and David Yarrow. Guardians of Safe Food. *Solstice,* No. 40, March 1990, pp. 14-21.

Marcus, Frances Frank. Drought Adds a Victim: Oyster Crop. *New York Times,* November 28, 1986.

Massachusetts Farm and Food System, The: A Five-Year-Policy Framework 1989-1993. Boston: Department of Food and Agriculture, The Commonwealth of Massachusetts, October 1988.

Mawby, Russell. Forward in Gordon Douglass, ed. *Cultivating Agricultural Literacy: Challenge for the Liberal Arts.* Battle Creek, MI: W.K. Kellogg Foundation. 2nd Edition, June 1985, p. 8.

McAfee, Noelle and Michael Waldman. Jim Hightower, Lone Star Rising. *Public Citizen,* July/August 1988.

McCullough, Rose and Daniel Weiss. An Environmental Look at the 1985 Farm Bill. *Journal of Soil and Water Conservation,* May/June, 1985.

Mellon, Margaret. Biotechnology, Human Disease and the FDA. Letter to *Science* 250, October 19, 1990, pp. 359-360.

Midwestern Legislative Conference of the Council of State Governments. See *Prodigal Crops.*

Molotsky, Irvin. Chicken Inspection Is Faulted. *New York Times,* May 13, 1987.

Morgan, Dan. *Merchants of Grain.* New York: Viking Press, 1979.

Nader, Laura. Energy and Equity: 'Magic, Science and Religion' Revisited. Paper presented at 51st ANZAAS (Australia New Zealand Association for the Advancement of Science) Congress, May 11, 1981, 27-page mimeo. + biblio.

Naess, Arne. Deep Ecology and Ultimate Premises. *The Ecologist* 18(4/5), 1988, pp. 128-131.

National Research Council (NRC). *Diet, Nutrition and Cancer.*

Washington, DC: National Academy Press, 1982.

_____. Board on Agriculture, Committee on the Role of Alternative Farming Methods in Modern Production Agriculture. *Alternative Agriculture*. Washington, DC: National Academy Press, 1989.

_____. See also Food and Nutrition Board.

Natural Resources Defence Council (NRDC). *Intolerable Risk: Pesticides in Our Children's Food*. New York: NRDC, February 27, 1989.

NCI to Spend $51 Million on Diet/Cancer Projects. *Nutrition Week*, May 18, 1989.

New Bacteria in the News: A Special Symposium. *Food Technology*, August 1987, pp. 16-26.

New Internationalist. Review of Andy Chetley's *The Politics of Baby Foods*, August 1986, p. 31.

New York State Council on Food and Nutrition Policy. *New York State Five Year Food and Nutrition Plan, 1988-1992*. Albany: New York State Department of Health, et al, n.d.

New York State Department of Health. 1986-87 Health Advisory on Contaminant Levels. Draft mimeo, May 19, 1986.

Nutraceuticals & Pharmafoods: The Food & Drug Interface. (Flyer for conference held January 24-25, 1991, New Orleans). Natick, MA: International Business Communications, 1990.

O'Neill, Molly. Eating to Heal: Mapping Out New Frontiers. *New York Times*, February 7, 1990, pp. C-1, C-6.

Osborn, Fairfield. *Our Plundered Planet*. Boston: Little, Brown, 1948.

Paddock, William and Paul Paddock. *Time of Famines*. Boston: Little, Brown, 1976.

Pahl, E. *Food Voting: Changing the Food System by Eating What Is Good for You and It*. Emmaus, PA: Cornucopia Project of Rodale Press, 1982, 22-page mimeo.

Papendick, Robert I., Lloyd F. Elliot and Robert B. Dahlgren. Environmental Consequences of Modern Production Agriculture: How Can Alternative Agriculture Address These Concerns? *American Journal of Alternative Agriculture* 1(1), Winter 1986.

Patterson, Blossom H. and Gladys Block. Food Choices and the Cancer Guidelines. *American Journal of Public Health* 78(3), March 1988, pp. 282-286.

Pear, Robert. Voters Spurn Array of Plans for Protecting Environment, *New York Times,* November 8, 1990.

Pennsylvania Food System, The: Crash or Self-reliance. Emmaus, PA: Cornucopia Project of Rodale Press, n.d., 22-page mimeo.

Perelmen, Michael. *Farming for Profit in a Hungry World.* Montclair, NJ: Allanheld, Osmun, 1977.

Perkins, John H. *Insects, Experts and the Insecticide Crisis.* New York and London: Plenum Press, 1982.

Perrow, Charles. *Normal Accidents.* New York: Basic Books, 1984.

Pimentel, D. *Food, Climate and Man.* New York: John Wiley, 1979.

Pimentel, D., M.S. Hunter, J.A. LaGro, R.A. Efroymson, J.C. Landers, F.T. Mervis, C.A. McCarthy and A.E. Boyd. Benefits and Risks of Genetic Engineering in Agriculture. *Bioscience* 39(9), 1989, pp. 606-614.

Pohl, Frederick and C. M. Kornbluth. *The Space Merchants* [1952]. New York: St. Martin's Press, 1985.

Pollack, Andrew. It May Taste Like Vanilla, But Is It Vanilla? *New York Times,* June 24, 1987, p 1.

Prodigal Crops: A Review of Proposals for Sustaining Agriculture. (Emerging Issues Series). A Report of the Midwestern Legislative Conference of the Council of State Governments, December 1988 (641 East Butterfield Road, Suite 401, Lombard, IL 60148).

Rasmussen, Clyde L. The Dynamic Food Industry and Our Eating Concepts. *Food Technology,* December 1965, pp. 36-44.

Reinhold, Robert. Drive Mounted for Environment Vote. *New York Times,* October 11, 1990.

Reiniccius, G. A. Flavor Safety. *Cereal Foods World* 34, June 1989, p. 487.

Rifkin, Jeremy. *Declaration of a Heretic.* Boston, and London: Routledge & Kegan Paul, 1985.

Right Livelihood Award, The. 1989 Right Livelihood Awards Focus on Medicine, Biodiversity, Economics and Native Rights. (Press Release). London, 1989.

Rizek, Robert L. Diets of American Women in 1985. *Food and Nutri-*

tion 61(1), January/February 1989, pp. 1-4.

Roberts, Leslie. l-Tryptophan Puzzle Takes New Twist. *Science* 249, August 31, 1990, p. 988.

Robertson, James. *The Sane Alternative: A Choice of Futures.* St. Paul, MN: River Basin Publishing, 1979.

Robinson, John P. The Time Squeeze. *American Demographics,* February 1990, pp. 30-33.

Rogoff, Marin H. and Stephen L. Rawlins. Food Security: A Technological Alternative. *Bioscience* 37(11), December 1987, pp. 800-808.

Rohlfing, Carla. Longevity's Latest Drugs: Milk, Carrots, Bread & OJ. *Longevity,* May 1990, pp. 34-38.

St. Louis, Michael E., Dale L. Morse, Morris E. Potter, Thomas M. Demelfi, John J. Guzewich, Robert V. Tauxe and Paul A. Blake. The Emergence of Grade A Eggs as a Major Source of *Salmonella Enteritidis* Infections. *Journal of the American Medical Association* 259, April 8, 1988, pp. 2103-2107.

Safe Food Action. 1(1), Fall 1989, p. 3.

Sale, Kirkpatrick. *Dwellers in the Land: The Bioregional Vision.* San Francisco: Sierra Club Books, 1985.

Schatan, Jacobo. *World Debt: Who Is to Pay?* London: Zed Books, 1987.

Schneider, Keith. Cloning Offers Factory Precision to the Farm. *New York Times,* February 17, 1988, pp. A1, D6.

Schneider, Keith. Betting the Farm on Biotech. *New York Times,* June 10, 1990a.

_____. Biotechnology Enters Political Race. *New York Times,* April 21, 1990b.

_____. F.D.A. Ruling Sought for Engineered Crops. *New York Times,* November 27, 1990c.

Schroth, M.N. and J.G. Hancock. Disease Suppressive Soil and Root Colonizing Bacteria. *Science* 216, June 25, 1982, pp. 1376-1381.

Schultz, Jack C. and I.T. Baldwin. Oak Leaf Quality Declines in Response to Defoliation by Gypsy Moth Larvae. *Science* 217, July 9, 1982, pp. 149-151.

Schutze, Jim. Hightower's View. *Organic Gardening,* December 1989.

Scientific American (Editorial), January 1990.

Seikatsu Club, The. Tokyo: Seikatsu Club Consumer Co-operative, 1988.

Shabecoff, Philip. Code of Pesticides Urged for Nation. Academy Report Sees a Peril of Cancer in the Food Supply. *New York Times,* May 21, 1987.

Shapiro, Eben. New Products Clog Food Stores. *New York Times,* May 29, 1990, pp. D-1, 17.

Shell Bacteria Kill East Coast Lobsters Near Ocean Dump. *New York Times,* May 22, 1988, pp. 1, 31.

Shopper Report, The. November 1990.

Shouldice, Rod. Personal Communication, June 1991.

Singer, Peter. *Animal Liberation*. New York: New York Review of Books, 1990.

Sinsheimer, Robert L. Social Implications of Genetic Engineering (Unpublished Speech), November 1981, 23-page mimeo.

Slater, Phillip. *The Wayward Gate*. Boston: Beacon Press, 1977.

Smith, Houston. Excluded Knowledge: A Critique of the Modern Western Mind Set. *Teachers College Record* 80 (3), February 1979, pp. 419-443.

Spahr, S. L. Milk products: Surplus or Shortage? Letter to *Science* 247, March 9, 1990, p. 1167.

Spika, John S., et al. Chloramphenicol-resistant *Samonella Newport* Traced Through Hamburger to Dairy Farms. *New England Journal of Medicine* 316(10), March 5, 1987, pp. 565-570.

Stableford, Brian. *Future Man*. New York: Crown Publishers, 1984.

Stalker, Peter. Sugarland: A Pastoral Visit to a Plantation. *New Internationalist,* No. 205, March 1990, pp. 14-15.

Stephens, George R., John Fleming, Linda Gacoin and Boris Bravo-Ureta. *Better Nutrition in Connecticut: Opportunities for Expanding Fresh Produce Production and Consumption* (Bulletin 852). New Haven: Connecticut Agricultural Experiment Station, January 1988.

Stipanovic, R.D. *The Function and Chemistry of Plant Trichomes and Glands on Insect Resistance*. Washington, DC: USDA Agricultural Research Service, 1982, 32 pp.

Sugarman, Carole. A Short Course in 'Organic' Chemistry. *Washington Post,* February 21, 1990.

Sun, Marjorie. Market Sours on Milk Hormone. *Science* 246, November 17, 1989, pp. 876-877.

Taylor, Lance. Interview: The Economics of Debt. *Multinational Monitor,* April 1990, pp. 17-20.

Tisserat, Brend, Carl E. Vandercook and Bark Berhow. Citrus Juice Vesicle Culture: A Potential Research Tool for Improving Juice Yield and Quality. *Food Technology,* February 1989, pp. 95-100.

Tudge, Colin. *The Famine Business.* London: Faber and Faber, 1977.

Ullrich, Helen. Editorial: The 'Plastic' World. *Journal of Nutrition Education* 4(1), Winter 1972, p. 4.

United States Department of Agriculture (USDA). *Report and Recommendations on Organic Farming.* Washington, DC: USDA, 1980.

_____. *Agricultural Adjustment Act of 1985.* Washington, DC: USDA, 1985.

United States Federal Trade Commission (FTC), *Natural and Organic Food Claims and Health and Related Claims.* Proposed Trade Regulation Rule of Food Advertising, 16 CFR Part 437, Phase 1. Staff Report and Recommendations. Washington, DC: FTC, September 25, 1978.

United States General Accounting Office (GAO). *Pesticides: Better Sampling and Enforcement Needed on Imported Food.* (Report No. GAO/RCED-86-219). Washington, DC: GAO, September 1986a.

_____. *Pesticides: Need to Enhance FDA's Ability to Protect the Public from Illegal Residues.* (Report No. GAO/RCED-87-7). Washington, DC: GAO, October 1986b.

_____. *Alternative Agriculture: Federal Incentives and Farmers Opinions.* Washington, DC: GAO, February 16, 1990a.

_____. *Biotechnology: Processing Delays Continue for Growing Backlog of Patent Applications.* Washington, DC: GAO, September 28, 1990b.

_____. *Federal Dairy Programs: Insights into Their Past Provide Perspectives on Their Future.* Washington, DC: GAO, February 1990c.

_____. *Food Safety and Quality: Who Does What in the Federal Government?* Washington, DC: GAO, December 1990d.

United States House of Representatives. Committee on Energy and Commerce. *Hard to Swallow: FDA Enforcement Program for Imported Food.* (Staff report by the Subcommittee on Oversight and Investigations). Washington, DC: U.S. Government Printing Office, July 1989.

_____. Committee on Government Operations. *Human Food Safety and the Regulation of Animal Drugs.* (House Report 99-461). Washington, DC: U.S. Government Printing Office, 1985.

United States Office of Technology Assessment (OTA). *Agricultural Postharvest Technology and Marketing Economics Research.* Washington, DC: U.S. Congress OTA, 1983.

Use of Plants as Bioreactors to Produce Recombinant Compounds Discussed. *Food Chemical News,* December 3, 1990, p. 28.

Vanilla and Biotechnology. Rural Advancement Fund International/ *Biocommunique,* January 1987.

Vanilla: Is It the Real Thing? *Africa Report,* September/October 1985.

Vaupel, Suzanne. Green initiative, broad environmental measure in California. *Organic Food Matters: The Journal of Sustainable Agriculture* II(2), Summer 1989, p. 14.

Vonnegut, Kurt, Jr. *Cat's Cradle.* New York: Dell Publishing, 1963.

Watkins, Alfred. *Till Debt Do Us Part: Who Wins, Who Loses and Who Pays for the International Debt Crisis.* Lanham, MD: University Press of America for the Roosevelt Center for American Policy Studies, 1986.

Weeds in Pest Management Systems. *California Agriculture* 36(7), July 1982, pp. 14-16.

Whiteside, Thomas. A Reporter at Large: Tomatoes. *The New Yorker,* January 24, 1977.

Whynott, Doug. Healthy Harvest. *Harrowsmith,* September/October 1989, pp. 32-41.

Wilford, John Noble. Moderate Drinking May Increase Risk of Cancer in Breast. *New York Times,* May 7, 1987, pp. 1, 25.

Wolff, Craig. Exxon Admits a Year of Breakdowns in S.I. Oil Spill. *New York Times,* January 10, 1990.

Youngberg, Garth. The Mainstreaming of Sustainable Agriculture. Speech to a special symposium on ecology and agriculture, Salina, Kansas, 1989. Mimeo.

Appendix
DIETARY GUIDELINES
FOR SUSTAINABILITY*

Joan Dye Gussow and Katherine L. Clancy

In the last few years, nutrition educators have begun asking increasingly sophisticated questions related to how to teach nutrition. Seeking to learn why people eat what they do and how better to teach them what we think they need or want to know, the profession has turned to models and theories from a variety of fields.[1,2,3] By contrast, new questions and understandings about what to teach have been generated almost entirely at the interface between nutrition and medicine by a concern over the relationship between diet and health. This is not surprising, since as Contento[4] has reminded us, the explicit goal of nutrition education has been to produce healthy and productive citizens.

We wish to argue here, however, that information on the relationship between human health and food choices is not a sufficient basis for nutrition education. In our time, educated consumers need to make food choices that not only enhance their own health but also contribute to the protection of our natural resources. Therefore, the content of nutrition education needs to be broadened and enriched not solely by medical knowledge, but also by information arising from disciplines

* Reprinted by permission of the authors from the *Journal of Nutrition Education* 18(1), 1986, pp. 1-5.

such as economics, agriculture and environmental science.

It is important to note that discussion of the implications—environmental, macroeconomic, and agricultural—of individuals' food choices has been widespread outside the nutrition community for a number of years, among groups with interests in subjects as diverse as vegetarianism, organic agriculture, community building, "natural healing," cooperatives, bioregionalism and social justice. But while individual nutritionists have worked with such groups, there appears as yet to have been no recognition by the profession that food choices might regularly be made not merely in terms of their nutritional impact on the individual but in terms of their impact on the long-term stability of the food system.

Nutritionists and the Food System

The notion that nutrition education ought in some way to be linked to agriculture and global resource issues is a very old one. Although most present-day professionals are young enough to be surprised by the fact, the earliest U.S. food guides, as Haughton (see Note 1) has pointed out, clearly reflected a concern with the food supply as well as with consumer health. In the early part of the century, pioneer nutritionist Henry Sherman was urging the purchase of locally produced fruits and vegetables to save energy and transportation costs, the use of grains to feed humans rather than livestock, and the substitution of dairy products for meat since the former were less wasteful of resources.[5]

Concern for the resource costs of our food choices is validated not only by our own history but by another traditional interest of nutritionists—world hunger. We are all familiar with the existence of hunger in various parts of the world, as we are with the conviction that—at least in emergencies—the U.S., with all its abundance, ought to be feeding the poor. It is our lack of attention to global resource issues that has allowed us to ignore the fact that the poor, especially in the developing countries, are actually feeding us.[6] Since we are rich enough to outbid the citizens of the Third World for the products of their own soils, we have become the largest food importer in the world. Moreover, our food demands are having an increasingly adverse effect on the natural resource base and the food self-reliance of poor countries.[7]

The concern that our diets may inadvertently contribute to the hunger of others is also not a new idea among some U.S. nutritionists; in fact, 36 years ago Sherman commented on this subject. Urging that consumers spend less of their food money on resource-intensive meat, he noted that "wide disparities of purchasing power and the willingness of many consumers to compete at high prices . . . tend to put serious strains upon good will and social justice between the 'haves' and 'have nots,' both within the nation and among the nations. With increasing knowledge . . . increasing numbers of people may give more open-minded thought to the possibility of some moderation of [demand] for foods which are inherently expensive of resources of product."[8] It is sobering to note that in the 20 years following Sherman's admonition, U.S. per capita beef consumption almost doubled, and the disparities between the world's haves and have nots increased.[9, 10]

Sustainable Agriculture

It is the latter trend away from economic justice that has led many groups currently recommending resource-conserving diets to use terms such as "just" or "responsible" to describe the food patterns they recommend. While these terms, with their implied moral assertion, are appropriate in some settings, we prefer for nutrition education a term that makes clear the scientific basis for considering the resource costs of dietary recommendations. We suggest . . . "sustainable diets" for what we propose, thus relating it to "sustainable agriculture," a concept that has been developing over a number of years.[11, 12, 13] To "sustain" is to support in life and health; sustainability has come to be associated with anything capable of maintaining itself within natural systems into the foreseeable future. Thus a sustainable agriculture is one that uses human and natural resources to produce food and fiber in a manner that is conservative, that is, in a manner that is not wasteful of such finite resources as top soil, water and fossil energy.

Against such a standard, the present food system is not a success, since most conventional farming practices and many food processes are wasteful of resources and nutrients and have a negative impact on the resource base, not just of the U.S. but of the world. Many of these adverse changes can be traced back to 1859 when we began to use, as if it were limitless, the finite supply of oil originally laid down over many millions of years. Fossil fuels such as oil can be converted into nitrogen fertilizers, pesticides and herbicides. [T]hey can be used to drive heavy machinery and pumps that push ground water into irrigation canals. Fossil fuels can also provide refrigeration and motive power to transport food from one area of the world to another.

The availability of cheap fossil fuels led U.S. farmers to depend heavily on all these inputs, producing an agricultural system that is energy inefficient [and] geographically concentrated [as well as] highly vulnerable to a variety of supply disruptions, biological surprises (e.g., pesticide resistance in insects and weeds), resource exhaustion (e.g., ground water depletion) and so on. Processors have been led down the same high-energy road, creating a food system in which for every calorie that comes to the table, 10 calories have been expended. Foods are subjected, postharvest, to a variety of processes, many of which use fossil energy while they remove indigenous nutrients. These problems, merely indicated here, have been explored in depth in a number of recent books.[14, 15, 16]

How can nutritionists incorporate the idea of sustainability into their teaching about food choices? The general suggestions to be made are obvious. Consumers should choose minimally processed and minimally packaged foods[17] and, when possible, buy locally produced foods to support regional agriculture that preserves farmland and that is less energy intensive. But how does such general advice get translated into actual dietary guidance? Haughton's suggestions for constructing a food guide for the year 2020 (Note 1) have not yet been translated into specific food-selection recommendations. We are aware of only one attempt to relate a specific food guide, in this case the Dietary Goals, to environmentally sensitive food selection (Note 2).

Sustainable Food Choices

Within the nutrition community there appears to be widespread adoption of the [USDA] *Dietary Guidelines*[18] as the basis for nutritional counseling aimed at promoting health. [W]e propose that nutritionists begin to use that same framework to address issues of sustainability. If such an idea has merit, it clearly deserves considerably more detailed attention than we can devote to it here. Therefore, the suggestions that follow are intended to initiate a discussion of the appropriateness of incorporating sustainability into our food guides:

(1) *Eat a variety of foods.* A primary reason for recommending variety in the diet is that when food selection draws on biological diversity, nutritional requirements are likely to be fully met. The proliferating "variety" in the supermarkets does not reflect an equivalent biological variety, since so many of the hundreds of available products are made from the same relatively few raw food materials.

What is perhaps less well known is that the biological base from which these thousands of novel products are made is actually narrowing. The human race once enjoyed a diet drawn from a large variety of plant and animal (including insect!) life. Now the world's population depends on a mere handful of species (30 to be exact), with four crops (wheat, rice, corn and potatoes) contributing more tonnage to the world total than the next 26 species combined.[19] Even more disturbing, the variety within those species is declining rapidly. In our own state of New York, only a few of the many varieties of apples that were formerly grown are available. In the U.S. there are 197 varieties of certified corn, but 60 percent of the crop comes from only four varieties.[20] Many people have called attention to the risks we face in allowing the world's population to become dependent on a few species of a few profitable crops.[19, 21] Thus nutritionists must help consumers learn to create a demand for a wider variety of whole foods instead of a succession of food novelties whose claim to diversity is based on processing techniques and artificial colors and flavors.

But promoting variety to the affluent sometimes has negative environmental consequences. Although the introduction of such exotic commodities as frogs' legs and palm hearts into the diets of the well-to-do may at first glance be praised as adding biological diversity, the energy and other costs of such novelty are often unacceptably high. Out-of-season produce, for example, is amazingly energy intensive. The calculated cost of flying one five-calorie strawberry from California to New York is 435 calories.[22] It is somewhat more complicated to calculate the energy, environmental, and other costs of producing a can of palm hearts by destroying a mature Brazilian wild palm or of consuming the legs from a frog that might otherwise have protected an Indian rice crop from insects.[23] So the variety we urge must be rational, seasonal and preferably local, with urgent attention given to the costs in natural and human resources of our more exotic demands.

(2) *Maintain ideal weight.* To overconsume calories is to waste food. In 1978, two professors calculated that the caloric difference between the actual weight of the population and its total ideal body weight was equivalent to the energy in 1.3 billion gallons of gasoline.[24] What would be added to that figure in wasted energy if one could count the calories lost and then regained on fad diets? It is at least worth asking ourselves whether an appeal to avoid the waste of overconsumption for the good of the planet might be more effective than appeals to purely selfish motives.

(3) *Avoid too much fat, saturated fat and cholesterol.* Even if there

were no demonstrated relationship between lipids and disease, there would still be compelling reasons for decreasing intake of foods rich in these compounds. Animal products, especially beef, are a major source of fat in the U.S. diet (meat, poultry, fish and dairy products [excluding butter] contribute 46 percent of the total fat and 58 percent of the saturated fatty acids in the diet),[25] and animal foods are not energy efficient. Although there is argument over how much grain it takes to produce how much beef, the Pimentels[22] have calculated that it takes over 29,000 kilocalories expended along the food chain to bring 375 kilocalories of beef to the table. In that sense, animals are an energy sink.

Energy waste is not the only price. Both here and abroad, cattle feeding is responsible for much environmental stress. A large percentage of U.S. cropland is used in growing feed grains, and production of such row crops is associated in many places with unsustainably high levels of soil erosion. LeVeen[26] states that the drop in per capita consumption of beef in the last decade reduced the consumption of corn and other feeds by about 500 million bushels, the equivalent of production from about 7.5 million acres of land.

Some suggest that cattle are less environmentally destructive if you simply let them graze. This suggestion ignores at least two facts: that cattle grazing on federal forests and rangelands are turning vast areas into deserts or near-deserts; and that Latin American tropical forests are being destroyed to create pastures for beef that will end up in U.S. fast-food restaurants.[27]

Another significant portion of our dietary fat comes from whole milk products, the output of a diary system that is supported by large sums of public money to produce a large surplus of high-fat dairy products. Since low-fat milk products are an important source of many nutrients, consumption of these products might well have been maintained more successfully than it has been had the industry acknowledged the need to decrease the fat content of all parts of the diet. However, dairy producers are paid according to the fat content of their milk. One can speculate that fabricated products such as imitation coffee whitener, imitation cheese and imitation margarine might never have been invented (or needed) had the fat-contributing portion of the diet been kept in balance.

(4) *Eat foods with adequate starch and fiber.* A major source of fiber in the diet is whole grains. However, many of the foods people eat in excess are made from refined grains that have lost their fiber as well as a large proportion of their indigenous nutrients. Most of what hap-

pens to grain after it leaves the farm profits the middlemen: the refiners and food manufacturers, the shippers and retailers.[28] There is no value to the farmer, to the maintenance of agriculture or to the biological variety of the diet when the refined grain fraction is converted into hundreds of products high in fat and salt or sugar.

Fruits and vegetables are other major sources of starch and fiber; however, as we suggested earlier in discussing "variety," all fruits and vegetables are not created equal where environmental impact is concerned. Until about 40 years ago, locally produced fruits and vegetables were major sources of vitamin C, fiber and other nutrients. But the role of locally produced commodities has been greatly reduced due to the "comparative advantage" in producing fruits, vegetables and nuts that California and a few other states have gained through access to cheap energy and subsidized water. Even though the transportation costs are high and even though for the same energy cost twice as much vitamin C can be produced by growing tomatoes as by growing oranges,[22] it is difficult for growers in places like New England to compete. This problem is only compounded by the "cash crop" fruits and vegetables that developing countries send us in order to earn precious foreign exchange.[6] Since the production of a wide variety of fruits and vegetables is more economical if the farmers have nearby outlets for their produce, direct markets of various kinds should be encouraged and patronized.

(5) *Avoid too much sugar.* Even if sugar supplied nutrients in addition to refined carbohydrates, even if it did not cause dental caries and . . . did not displace other nutrients form the diet, it would still be difficult to rationalize the use of 6,000 kilocalories of energy just to process one kilogram of beet sugar that supplied only 3,800 kilocalories to the consumer. But substituting saccharin or aspartame in a diet soft drink is not the ecological bargain it first appears to be, since the 1 kilocalorie comes packaged in an aluminum can that takes 1,600 kilocalories to produce.

(6) *Avoid too much sodium.* Since it is processing that adds salt to foods, the selection of fresh or minimally processed foods promotes both sustainability and health. But there is another "salt" problem worth discussing, since it provides an excellent illustration of the fact that not all the food production problems can be addressed through diet.

Of the close to 12 million acres of cropland in California, 10 million are irrigated and, of these, close to 3 million have accumulated various salts from irrigation water to a level that interferes with production.[29] One proposed solution to the salinity problem of these soils is to breed crops "tolerant" of high salt levels. Although adequate research has not yet been conducted to determine whether salt-tolerant plants will contain somewhat higher sodium levels, the salt solution will need to be very carefully designed. And here nutritionists might find themselves more engaged with water subsidy legislation than with traditional nutrition education efforts.

(7) *Drink alcoholic beverages only in moderation.* There are other reasons besides cirrhosis to drink alcoholic beverages only in moderation. While the energy inputs for processing of wine, spirits and beer are much lower than those for sugar,[22] the total energy requirements for production, processing and packaging are much greater.[30] For products which have almost no food value and can be toxic as well, the environmental and health costs are high.

Discussion

The preceding are but a few of the reasons why it seems appropriate to build major educational programs around dietary guidelines for a sustainable diet. In both our agricultural and food processing systems, we are wasting our own natural resources and those of countries poorer than ours. On a worldwide scale, the system is functioning so as to threaten our future food supply. But because the problem is difficult to see and because the connections between an imported winter fruit and soil erosion 2,000 miles away are difficult to make, consumers, like producers, have not understood how to act in their own self-interest.[31] The economics of the system are failing to produce sustainability.

Therefore, while we wait for some unavoidable crisis to arise within the food system that might lead to a change in the practices of the agro-food industry, we must turn to the final arbiter of the food system: the consumer. The [USDA] *Dietary Guidelines* are helping us teach consumers about health. We are proposing here that they can at the same time be used to help teach consumers about the food system and its sustainability.

As we hope this discussion has made clear, to take account of sustainability within the framework of the *Dietary Guidelines* will mean that all sources of nutrients will not be viewed as equally desirable. If the "goodness" of certain foods is viewed as deriving from more than their nutrient content, consumer demand would increase for foods produced in certain ways and in certain locations.

Such choices, even the suggestion that such choices ought to be made, of course will cause controversy, just as the suggestion that consumers ought to eat less fat has caused vociferous objections in certain producer circles. The reality is that the actions of nutrition educators always have political ramifications, even if they are often unintended.

It is clear that sustainable diets, even if widely adopted, will not lead automatically to a sustainable agriculture. What is required for widespread adoption of the latter is a farm policy that rewards agricultural practices conserving of natural resources, and an overall policy (domestic and foreign) that promotes regional self-reliance in food both here and abroad. Such a policy shift cannot be generated by farmers alone, since less than 3 percent of the people in this country are now farming, or even by those presently concerned with either domestic or foreign agricultural policy, since that constituency is a very small one. It can be hoped, however, that nutritionists who become concerned about how the food they recommend has been produced will become natural allies of those who wish to grow and process food in a manner consistent with the long-term stability of the food system.

NOTES

1. Haughton, B. The Cosmopolitan Radish: Procedures for Constructing a Food Guide for New York City and State in the Year 2020. Unpublished Ed.D. dissertation, Teachers College, Columbia University, New York, 1982.
2. Mottern, N. Guidelines for Food Purchasing in the United States. Winchester, Virginia, 1978, 201 pp.

LITERATURE CITED

1. Brun, J., ed. *Nutrition Education Research: Strategies for Theory Building.* Rosemont, IL: National Dairy Council, 1981, 166 pp.
2. Sims, L., and L. Light. *Directions for Nutrition Education Research—The Penn State Conferences—& Proceedings.* University Park, PA: Pennsylvania State University and U.S. Department of Agriculture, 1980, 108 pp.
3. Olson, C., and A. Gilespie, eds. Proceedings of the Workshop on Nutrition Education Research. *Journal of Nutrition Education* 13 (Supp. 1), 1981, 118 pp.
4. Contento, I. Thinking About Nutrition Education: What to Teach, How to Teach it, and What to Measure. *Teachers College Record* 81, 1980, pp. 421-447.
5. Sherman, H. Permanent Gains from the Food Conservation Move-

ment. *Columbia University Quarterly* 21, 1919, pp. 1-19.

6. George, S. *Ill Fares the Land—Essays on Food, Hunger, and Power.* Washington, DC: Institute for Policy Studies, 1984, 102 pp.

7. Oxfam America. Food Exports from the Third World: Senegal: Opening the Road to Hunger. *Facts for Action* 11, 1984.

8. Sherman, H. *The Nutritional Improvement of Life.* New York: Columbia University Press, 1950, p. 64.

9. Economic Research Service, USDA. *U.S. Food Consumption, Sources of Data and Trends, 1909-1963.* Statistics Bulletin 364, GPO 778-610. Washington, DC: USDA, 1965, 194 pp.

10. Economic Research Service, USDA. *Food Consumption, Prices and Expenditures.* Agricultural Economics Report 138. (1977 Supp.), Washington, DC: USDA, 1979, 97 pp.

11. Jackson, W., W. Berry and B. Colman, eds. *Meeting the Expectations of the Land.* San Francisco: North Point Press, 1984, 250 pp.

12. Besson, J.M., and H. Yogtmann, eds. *Towards a Sustainable Agriculture.* Oberwill, Switzerland: Verlag Wirz AG, 1978, 243 pp.

13. Knorr, D., ed. *Sustainable Food Systems.* Westport, CT: AVI Publishing, 1984, 416 pp.

14. Busch, L., and W. Lacy, eds. *Food Security in the United States.* Boulder, CO: Westview Press, 1984, 430 pp.

15. Knorr, D., and T. Watkins, eds. *Alterations in Food Production.* New York: Van Nostrand Reinhold, 1984, 241 pp.

16. Haynes, R., and R. Lanier. *Agriculture, Change and Human Values, Proceedings of a Multidisciplinary Conference.* Gainesville, FL: Humanities and Agriculture Program, 1982, 1,176 pp.

17. Knorr, D., and K. Clancy. Safety aspects of processed foods. In: Busch and Lacy, eds, *Food Security, op. cit.,* pp. 231-253.

18. U.S. Department of Agriculture and Department of Health and Human Services. *Dietary Guidelines for Americans.* Home and Garden Bulletin No. 232. Washington, DC: U.S. Government Printing Office, 1980, 20 pp.

19. Harlan, J. The Plants and Animals that Nourish Man. *Scientific American* 235, 1976, pp. 88-97.

20. Butler, L. J. Issues and Perspectives in Plant Breeding. In: Busch and Lacy, eds, *Food Security, op. cit.,* pp. 284-327.

21. Merrill, R. Toward a Self-sustaining Agriculture. In: R. Merrill, ed., *Radical Agriculture,* New York: Harper Colophon Books, 1976, pp. 284-327.

22. Pimentel, D., and M. Pimentel. *Food, Energy and Society.* New York: John Wiley, 1979, 164 pp.

23. Heart Torn Out of Wild Palm Trees. *Mazingira* 8(3), July 1984, p. 12; and R. Rao. Frog Deaths Threaten Indian Rice Crops. *Mazingira* 8(1), p. 8.

24. Hannon, B., and T. Lohman. The Energy Cost of Overweight in the United States. *American Journal of Public Health* 68, 1978, pp. 765-769.

25. Marston, R., and S. Welsh. Nutrient Content of the U.S. Food Supply, 1982. *National Food Review* NFR-25 USDA-ERS, pp. 1-13.

26. LeVeen, P. Domestic Food Security and Increasing Competition for Water. In: Busch and Lacy, eds. *Food Security, op. cit.,* pp. 61-98.

27. Fradkin, P. The Eating of the West. *Audubon,* January 1979, pp. 94-121; and Sequeira, M. Costa Rica: Green Alternative. *Multinational Monitor* 5(7), July 1984, p. 8.

28. Buttel, F. Agriculture, Environment and Social Change; Some Emergent Issues. In: F. Buttel and H. Newby, eds., *The Rural Sociology of the Advanced Societies—Critical Perspectives,* Montclair, NJ: Allanheld, Osmun, 1980, pp. 453-486.

29. Backlund, V., and R. Hoppes. Status of Soil Salinity in California. *California Agriculture* 38(10), October 1984, pp. 8-9.

30. Green, M. *Eating Oil: Energy Use in Food Production.* Boulder, CO: Westview Press, 1978, 205 pp.

31. Gussow, J. Food: Wanting, Needing and Providing. *Food Monitor* 34, 1983, pp. 12-15.